# sharing our prayers

# sharing our prayers

## 12 Testimonies on Spiritual Habits to Improve Your Life

### SHANI MCILWAIN

**SHARING OUR PRAYERS**
Published by Purposely Created Publishing Group™
Copyright © 2018 Shani McIlwain

All rights reserved.

No part of this book may be reproduced, distributed or transmitted in any form by any means, graphics, electronics, or mechanical, including photocopy, recording, taping, or by any information storage or retrieval system, without permission in writing from the publisher, except in the case of reprints in the context of reviews, quotes, or references.

Printed in the United States of America
ISBN: 978-1-947054-64-6

---

Special discounts are available on bulk quantity purchases by book clubs, associations and special interest groups. For details email: sales@publishyourgift.com or call (888) 949-6228.

*For information logon to:*
www.PublishYourGift.com

To all the prayer warriors in my life.

# Table of Contents

Acknowledgments .................................... 1

Introduction ....................................... 3

Jesus and Me ....................................... 5
*Rev. Bernice Parker-Jones*

Prayer Works ...................................... 15
*Tonya Barbee*

Faith on Fleek .................................... 23
*LuDrean Peterson*

A Spiritual Recess ................................ 33
*Marian Currie*

Forever in My Heart ............................... 43
*Ruby Mabry*

Death Brought Me Life ............................. 51
*Milton Dickerson*

Forgive! Live Through It, Grow Through It ......... 59
*Rev. Allison G. Daniels*

The Fallout of Prayer ............................. 69
*Roz Knighten-Warfield*

A Daughter's Prayer from Fear to Faith ............... 79
*Tina Mayo-Hunter*

Father-Daughter Relationship ...................... 87
*Veronica Howard*

Get In Agreement .................................. 95
*Yolanda Douthit*

About the Authors ............................... 105

Sources ......................................... 117

# Acknowledgments

I would like to thank each coauthor who took the time to partner with me in sharing a piece of themselves with the world. My heart is overflowing with the love, time, and tears put into this project.

Thank you!

# Introduction

Prayer is the communication between ourselves and God, but it's not as serious or formal as we may think. We should look at prayer as just a conversation between two friends. I write about prayer because I find that most of our issues are results of our not having an active prayer life.

This book is for anyone who has ever felt alone or tired while dealing with a life-altering problem or trial test, or may have forgotten the power of prayer. I pray that everyone who has the opportunity to read this book is blessed, restored, reminded that God is living and wants to be an active participant in your life.

Throughout this book, there will be prompts instructing you to reflect on something that has happened in your own life and write a prayer about it. When you write, you remember: like I said before, many times, you forget the power of prayer, so writing things down reminds us of what we have gone through and gets us over the next test.

I am so grateful to my coauthors, co-teachers, and leaders who have taken the time to share their wisdom.

Let's get started!

Shani McIlwain

# Jesus and Me

*He Knelt Down in Prayer Beside Me*

## REV. BERNICE PARKER-JONES

My grandmother, who I called Momma, was a praying woman. I'd listen to her as she'd sit rocking back and forth in her old rocking chair, talking to God. Her praying posture was different than most. She didn't close her eyes or kneel down beside the bed. She just rocked and prayed, and sometimes sang. One of her favorite songs was "You Can't Make Me Doubt Him." Day in and day out, she could be heard singing or humming that song as she rocked.

This was perhaps my first introduction to the power of prayer, though I didn't realize it until I was much older. Unbeknownst to me, I learned to pray, not by following a prescribed formula, but by watching the example of someone who prayed consistently. From this living example, I also gleaned what prayer can do in the life of the one offering the prayer.

I did not always pray. Sometimes I did a "drive-thru prayer" as I'd run out the door or crawl into bed. If I'm being truthful, all those years ago, I used to have a problem with my grandmother's singing and praying all the time. She had broken her hip during a fall and was never able to walk again, but she never let her lack of mobility stop her from praising God. I, on the other hand, questioned how she could believe in a God who could not heal her.

But then the day came when I had to put all my observations from Momma into practice. I needed help. I had just taken my three-year-old daughter to spend the summer with her grandparents in Virginia. When time came for me to pick her up, I had neither transportation nor money. As I think back on that time in my life, I had fallen into a well of depression and was sinking further and further into the abyss. I only had enough strength to go to work and sleep, and even those tasks were made challenging by my awful migraine headaches. I was not on the Lord's side, but He certainly was on mine.

It was during one of those dark nights of my soul that I tried prayer. Depressed, crying, and at the end of my rope, I lay prostrate on my bedroom floor and called out to Jesus for help. Some Christians would say that, as believers, we're not supposed to be depressed. Of course, I beg to differ with that philosophy. Depression for me was being in the state of not caring about anything and being overwhelmed with a feeling of uselessness—no purpose. My life had no meaning and I felt like a fish out of water. I thought I'd been praying all my life and that I was getting no results. Where was Momma's God when I needed Him?

But on that night, as I lay in my bedroom, there was a shift. Luke 22:44 records that, when Jesus was in agony in the Garden of Gethsemane, He experienced hematohidrosis, "and being in anguish, he prayed more earnestly, and his sweat was like drops of blood falling to the ground" (NIV). My experience was certainly not as intense as Jesus', but my prayer life changed that night. I was no longer driving through the fast-prayer lane—I was toiling at the foot of the cross. It was at that point that I felt a strange presence beside me; not speaking, but just there. I concluded that Momma's God had come to my rescue. He knelt down and met me at my point of need. I learned the power of prayer and some things that prayer could do.

First, prayer is a sustainer. I had not yet learned that, in praying, you might not get all you ask for externally; but there's the power of God at work on the inside that gives you peace of mind and steadfastness. When you pray aright, prayer sustains you. I guess Momma, who could not read the Bible, had learned to apply Paul's principle about contentment found in Philippians 4:11: "I have learned in whatever situation I am to be content" (NIV). Contentment is when you know that God is able to hold you up under any pressure. Prayer will keep you grounded and hold you together, even when the world around you is falling apart. As Tramaine Hawkins' song says,

"When you pray, everything will be alright; just have faith." Another key point: faith is an essential element in praying. The measure of faith initially given to me continues to grow incrementally as my relationship with God grows. So, if you want to find peace and contentment, be bold and faithful in your prayer life. God will sustain you.

God sustained Momma during the many years she was confined to that old rocking chair. Prayer was not an option for her. It was who she was; it was what she did all day and in the wee hours of the night. And three-score-plus years later, I've learned to pray for myself and I understand it better, by and by. I now know that, without her committed prayer life, Momma's life would have been hard to bear. But unlike me who became extremely disappointed in the fact that God did not heal her physically, she seemed always at peace.

Another lesson I've learned is that prayer will strengthen you for the journey. One morning, I was working out on my treadmill. Out of breath and legs feeling too heavy to make another step, I was ready to quit. I was pushing for two miles and determined to burn 350 calories. So, I started repeating Philippians 4:13: "I can make it through anything in the One who makes me who I am" (MSG). The treadmill was getting the best of me and I had a "give-up" mindset. Nevertheless, I continued speaking that verse, this time from the King James Version: "I can do all things through Christ who strengthens me."

The more I said it, the louder I said it and with more conviction. I kept repeating it over and over until I was literally shouting it out (I'm glad I was home alone). The Holy Spirit began to minister to me, encouraging me that I could push through. Sometimes, when we become weary or the journey seems too hard to bear, we quit too soon. Instead of quitting, I encourage you to PUSH: Pray Until Something Happens. Turn your prayer into praise for we know that God inhabits the praises of His people.

This brings us to our third and final lesson: our prayer language makes us beings of prayer and praise. Prayer, as Richard Foster says in his book *Disciples of the Spirit*, is a discipline, not a ritual. It can happen anywhere, but I've discovered that there's nothing like finding that quiet place where you and Jesus can kneel together and commune as friends.

The War Room Bible Study suggests a quiet place for prayer, a prayer closet where we take all our concerns to God in prayer. I agree: this is my meeting place with God. This is where I commune with Him, bringing my fragmented life. Jesus Himself often traveled to quiet places to spend time with God the Father (Luke 5:16). I personally like to withdraw to the quiet of my sunroom to just sit and listen. This quiet time with God evokes within me a peace that surpasses all understanding. It gives me opportunity to talk with God and to listen. Sometimes, I probably talk too much and do not listen enough. Since prayer is a two-way communication between God and me, I need to practice the art of listening. In listening, I hear the answer to my prayer: sometimes it's "yes," sometimes "no," and other times "not yet." As a child, I was told that I may not get all I want, but my every need would be taken care of. So, in my walk with the Lord, I'm learning to trust that God knows what's best for me and will supply all my needs according to his riches in glory.

Sometimes, when I am preparing to go into a season of specified prayer—in other words going into my personal "War Room"—God puts this song in my spirit: "There are days I'd like to be all alone with Christ, my Lord, I can tell Him of my trouble all alone…There are days to fast and pray for the pilgrim in his way, there are days to be with Christ all along…" (G. T. Byrd). This hymn sets the tone and environment when entering into the centering prayer mood.

During these quiet moments, I am transformed, as Howard Thurman says in *The Centering Moment*, from performing the act of praying to becoming the *being* of prayer. It is during those awesome moments that I can feel His breath. This is when prayer ceases being an act; I truly become one with God, in His presence. I center my being on Him and commune with Him as friend. I give Him all the fragments of my life and trust that He will use those fragments to teach me valuable lessons, even as He is putting my life back together.

Looking back on my life—where God has brought me and to where He is taking me—I can truly say that I know that the prayers of the righteous avails. I am convinced that Momma prayed for me. I was somewhat on the wild side and, as a young adult, I was involved in some things I'm too ashamed to mention. I could and probably should have been in jail or addicted to drugs. That's how I know that my grandmother's prayers worked for me. God truly took all of my broken pieces and shaped me for His purpose.

I'm still a work in progress as I continue to learn to pray about everything, sometimes even after the fact. It's like taking that first bite of that yellow cake with chocolate frosting (my favorite), then realizing that I had not given thanks to God. Sometimes, I've started out on a journey in my life and said, "Oops, I forgot to pray." But I have learned to pray in season and out of season, when things are good and when things are bad. God has control over all.

Finally, I'll share another experience of how prayer sustained and strengthened me. In 2005, I had a major spinal surgery. During childbirth thirty-three years earlier, I was told that I had an abnormal S-shaped spine and was warned never to have surgery. Now, in the prime of my life, my spine had severely curved to the point that it was becoming increasingly more difficult for me to breath and walk. After seeking out several specialists, I met one who encouraged me to get surgery. I was scared, extremely scared. I remembered the advice from thirty-three-years earlier and thought I might be paralyzed if anything went wrong. This was a dark time for me.

As a minister of the Gospel, I'd lay hands on the sick in our church and many told me that they'd been healed after. I preached about having faith and trusting God even in the difficult and darkest hours. I encouraged others, but I could not encourage myself. Yes, I had been praying about my own situation, but was still scared. I shared my situation with only a few family members, and I even took my grandchildren to Disneyland just in case I became paralyzed. Finally, after several consultations with the spine surgeon and my family, I decided to trust God as my Healer.

I had been praying and preparing myself, physically and spiritually—or so I thought. Well, one night again, I fell prostrate before the Lord with my litany of questions, all beginning with "what if." What if I am paralyzed? What if I die during surgery? What if the anesthesiologist does not give me enough medicine and I wake up during the surgery? What if? What if? God's answer was consistently the same with each question: It's going to be all right. Again during that time of centering prayer, God knelt beside me and I felt His calming presence and assurance. I knew Him as my Sustainer, my Healer, and the One Who strengthens me.

The surgery was a long thirteen hours. I remained in intensive care for two days because I lost a significant amount of blood. But guess what? On the third day (there's something special about the third day), I was up and walking down the hallway, an inch taller because I no longer walked leaning to the side. My posture was straight! Listening to the doubters, I kept waiting for the pain to come, but I never had pain and refused the narcotics offered as pain relievers. It's been twelve and a half years and I'm still praising God for the healing and for my skilled surgeon. My prayer of thanksgiving becomes my praise.

In prayer, I take all my worries, fragments, disappointments, sorrows, and questions to God. I don't always leave them there, but that's my work in progress. Now, when people ask me to pray for them, I don't wait until I get home; I've been known to pray in the middle of parking lots or on street corners. I know that, when you pray, things do work out. Maybe not the way I want them to, but I trust that God knows best and I just wait.

It is in our committed prayer life that our relationship with God flourishes. Meet Him in your quiet place and He will kneel down beside me and breathe new life. God meets me at my point of need, and He will meet you at yours.

# Prayer Works

## TONYA BARBEE

I was dumbfounded. I didn't know how it happened to me, only that it did happen. I discovered that my husband married me while he was still married to someone else. Unbelievable! How did I miss the signs? What was I going to do? We have a son together and I made a vow to be married "till death do us part." But he had shared vows with another woman *way* before me and that's to whom he owes homage. My marriage of eight years was fraudulent. My wedding was not real. My life as I saw it fell apart.

When I found out he was still married to her, I asked him to leave my home immediately. . He tried to lie his way out of it but I no longer heard a word he said. He had and he did. All that I thought he was, he was not. He was not the Christian man I'd presumed he was.

I'm a single parent again. And our son—oh, how he loved his father. I could see it in his dark, brown eyes and in how he jumped up and down whenever his dad was in his presence. Our son was only seven at the time.

My heart burned with betrayal, anger, pain, resentment, and, most of all, sadness. But I knew I would soon have to forgive in order to move forward. I asked God to help me forgive. I needed to release the anger and resentment that was burning inside of me. I didn't want to hate men altogether because all men don't hurt women.

When he left, I had bills galore. Bills that he promised he would pay off when his new business venture launched. Well, every time he would be close to acquiring million-dollar funding, it would never come to fruition. Funding was eventually denied altogether. Nothing came through for him. Karma is for real. But the catch is that I too came close to losing everything I owned: my home, my SUV that he drove every day while I was at work, the utilities, my credit cards that I used to help fund his ventures and to stay afloat. It was all building up quicker than I could bat an eye. I thought I was going to lose my mind but that was not an option. I had an important job that worked closely with my company's president, I had to raise my son, and I had another teenager I needed to get into college. I had to pull it together and figure out a way to pay these bills.

God will help me. He will help me through this mess. I believed this but I was still frightened. My coworkers knew something was wrong because I was no longer my jovial self.

I was sad. I held my head down. I often cried at work. I was concerned about my son who'd just seen his parents separate. I even went to counseling. Soon, I realized that I needed Him. I got on my knees and prayed to God:

*God, I don't know how I'm going to get out of this mess except through You. You said that, through You, all things are possible for those who love You. I need You to give me the strength to pull it together. I need to manage my work responsibilities and get back to my 100%. I need to forgive this sick man for what he did to me and move on with my life. I also need You to get me through this debt so that I won't lose everything You've entrusted to me.*

*Father God, help me to land on my feet. In the name of Jesus, I pray, Amen.*

A friend of mine recommended I talk to his attorney, who was one of the top in the DMV area. He agreed to only charge me court-filing fees to take on my case, which would have otherwise cost me approximately $15,000 or more, since bigamy is hard to prove. Still, this powerful firm discovered the true facts and, within thirteen months, my marriage was annulled. A marriage of eight years was annulled, just like that. My girlfriend, who came with me to court, assured me that I would be fine because I'm a child of God. I felt like a conqueror. I knew that God was on my side and things would continue to move forward for me because, through it all, I always had a relationship with Him. I know He's the ruler over all things and that, through Him, all things are possible. I became empowered to get my life in order.

However, change did not come overnight. My SUV broke down. I hadn't driven it much since I had married my ex-husband, who would take me to work and pick me up everyday. I never knew whether or not he'd gotten the car serviced. He also had over $1500 of traffic tickets in D.C. where he apparently spent a lot of time, and I'd never known about any of them. He must have intercepted the mail too. After my car engine died, I had to buy another car. What happens when you have more bills than you have money? Your credit worsens. I chose a used car with 40,000 miles and I could only take it off the lot with an interest rate of twenty-six percent! Yes. Correct. You pay more in interest when your credit is bad.

I also had to work on saving my home. I was a few months behind on my mortgage payments so I did research on home modifications. After being three months behind, I was able to apply for a modification through my mortgage company and Maryland's HOPE program. They sent me at least ten forms to complete and, believe it or not, I had to send those same forms at least three different times through mail and fax. But I didn't give up. When you need something badly, you have to persevere.

Originally, they approved the modification for a few hundred dollars off. For me, it was still unaffordable. I prayed to God that they would reduce it more. I reapplied months later and, by the grace of God, they approved me for another modification half off the original mortgage payment and forgave $100,000 that I no longer have to pay back! The only catch was that, at the end of the loan, I'd have a balloon payment. But with $100k forgiven, I was confident I would be fine. Prayer, persistence, and perseverance paid off. I'm still in my home today. God is amazing!

A year later, a friend of mine asked me to meet him at a nearby officers' club on a military base. I was watching TV that evening and really didn't want to go but he sounded disappointed when I declined so I reluctantly got off the couch, took a shower, and got dressed in a red dress to meet him. He was there with a nice young lady he wanted me to meet. We all danced and had a great time. When my buddy left to get us drinks, this handsome, tall man came up to our table and asked me to dance. I danced with this smiling man most of the night. I felt safe with him and was compelled to talk to him on the dance floor, something I never did before. I yelled out to him over the large speakers to ask his name. I guessed that he was from the South because of his accent. I was correct.

We danced all night long to slow songs, fast songs, swinging to the beat on each song. I would go back and forth to check on my friend and his date, but eventually, my attention was reverted to this interesting man. I felt so good with him. He exuded strength and confidence. I decided after the seventh dance that he *had* to be my friend. I gave him my contact information as he walked me to my new, used car. I gave him every number and email I had. I felt compelled to have him in my life.

From thereon, we talked every night till the wee hours of each morning. I grew very fond of him although he was different than anyone I had ever dated. He told me he had raised his two girls by himself and I became even more attracted to him. Whereas I was a true extrovert, he was surely an introvert. But it didn't matter. I appreciated everything different about him. We went on many dates and we frequented that same military establishment where we first met.

One day, he came to visit me and, being a very perceptive man, he noticed that I was agitated. I told him I had some things to take care of but that I was good. He didn't accept what I said so I told him about the exorbitant bills. He said very abruptly, "I don't pay women's bills."

I replied, "I didn't ask you to."

In fact, I was taking a class at my church to help me learn how to manage God's resources. Did you know that all of our belongings actually belong to God? We are just stewards over what He has blessed us with. I was learning how to be a better steward in this class. One of the homework assignments was to write everything down from the highest bill to the lowest and I did that in an Excel spreadsheet.

My new friend asked to see my bills. I reluctantly brought down a huge kitchen trash bag full of unpaid bills. He looked discouraged as I came down the steps, but still asked to take a copy of the spreadsheet and left. I assumed I would never see him again and that he would burn wheelies on the pavement as he sped off, never looking back. There was over $7,500 worth of late bills on the spreadsheet. The majority was colored in red to illustrate outstanding bills. Those highlighted in green were paid in full and those in yellow showed I made arrangements to pay.

I prayed that he would remain my friend even though my financial situation looked unappealing. Within thirty minutes of leaving my home, he called me. I thought he was going to say, "I ain't never coming back to see you." But, it was just the opposite: he was on his way back to talk to me. When he walked in, he asked me if I had electronic access to my bills. I did. He asked that I retrieve them one-by-one. He pulled out his debit card while we sat in my dining room table and he paid them one-by-one until his bank shut down his card. That didn't deter him. He called his bank, identified himself, and kept going.

God is amazing. I had just surrendered my bills to Him, and He responded in the form of my friend. Remember, my friend had never done this before. But that's how God works: He sends those to do His work, to assure you that He's in your life.

That was five years ago. Since then, I've become a better steward over God's gifts to me and my credit score went from 500 to the mid-700s. My friend is now my loving partner. God blessed me with someone who is respectful, honest, and an upstanding role model for my son.

I was once scared. I felt betrayed. I was lost. But I always knew that God has the final say. I know that we are meant to go through challenges—they are a part of life and it's not always going to be easy. But we aren't supposed to give up when things seem disastrous. We aren't supposed to close up to the world. We're supposed to get through it.

Trust that God will be with us throughout. I'm at peace now and I have forgiven all who have hurt me. I have learned to put my faith in God and Him alone.

# Faith on Fleek

*The Doctors Could Not Understand
What My Faith Could Feel*

LUDREAN PETERSON

*That your faith should not stand in wisdom of men,
but in the power of God.*

—1 Corinthians 2:5

I am a child of God. I stand on a solid foundation that is built on faith. My outlook on life used to depend on trying to make sense and logic of every single thing. But today, I start my morning as I end my night: thanking and praising God, asking Him to allow me to do His will.

Over the years, I have experienced and witnessed some things that neither science nor common sense can fathom. When the unexplainable and illogical happens, you know that God and Jesus are in the midst and you keep the faith. I was once faced with a health scare, a severe case of anemia. The doctor's couldn't understand what my faith could feel.

It was time for my annual physical. In the past, Kaiser Permanente normally requested that I have blood work done two days prior to my scheduled visit. However, when I called to confirm my appointment and asked about the red blood count, I was informed that they changed their policy and no longer required it. Being anemic, I have a history of a low blood count, and it is imperative that I frequently have my blood levels checked.

Months prior to my doctor's visit, I had been eating an outrageous amount of ice. A craving of ice is a sign of iron deficiency. I even engaged in a number of social media threads regarding which restaurants and locations have the best ice. It dawned on me that I had grown addicted to ice (side note: ice lovers, make sure you go and get your iron levels checked, especially if you're having cravings several times a day or if it's out of control). It had also been a while since I had taken my iron pills. Given all this information, I already had it set in my mind that, once I got to my doctor's office, I would request that blood work be done.

The day of my scheduled physical arrived and I was prepared, as usual, with a list of questions and updates outlined to discuss with my doctor. I also wanted to get a referral to see a specialist. I completed multiple appointments with various doctors in the center and went on my merry way. So far, so good, everything was fine—or so I thought.

I wasn't ready for the series of events that were about to occur the next day. I went to work and was at my second meeting of the day when my telephones began to ring back to back. First my personal cell phone, next my work cell phone, and then my work office phone. When I noticed that all of the calls were from the same number, I excused myself from the meeting and answered the phone. The voice on the other line said, "This is Kaiser and we have an emergency. You need you to come in right away. Please confirm your date of birth…"

I asked what this call was about because I had just seen multiple doctors. They confirmed that it was regarding my blood work. They informed me that I would need to alert my family members to let them know that I would likely be transported from Kaiser to the hospital to have an emergency blood transfusion. More specifically, my blood count was critically low and had fallen to 6.2. Being anemic, my normal number is 9.4. The normal for most people is 15. Due to my low number, I had to take iron supplements.

I asked to speak with my primary doctor and was informed that she was on leave and unreachable for the remainder of the day. The choice of words used during the call were strong enough to put fear in anyone, but I wasn't shaken.

> *Do not fear, for I am with you.*
> *Do not be dismayed, for I am God.*
>
> — **Isaiah 41:10**

One thing that I have always appreciated about being an employee of the Food and Drug Administration is that I get to work with doctors and scientists. Whenever my family or I am faced with medical issues, I can pretty much talk to my coworkers and ask them about the details of a situation. For this instance, I went to my supervisor, who is an internal medicine doctor and former employee of Kaiser, and gave her an overview of my call. She gave me the worst and best case scenarios and explained the seriousness of the matter. During the discussion with my supervisor, I explained my concern of being called in by another doctor while my primary doctor was unavailable. I felt uneasy about having new doctors reviewing my information and just going off of my current blood count without knowledge of my history.

My supervisor understood and explained to me the questions they were going to ask and what I should expect once I got at Urgent Care. When I arrived, they checked my pulse and my vitals to make sure they were fine (they were). The doctor came in to introduce himself and proceeded to go over the results of my blood work. With a concerned look on his face, he explained how vitally low my numbers were. He looked at the numbers on the computer screen, looked at me, and then he looked at the numbers on the screen again. He put his hand on his chin and looked in disbelief and stated, "This is unbelievable. You don't look like what your number reports. Basically, based on your number, you should be passed out or unconscious. You should be experiencing a shortness of breath. You shouldn't even be able to think coherently."

Based on my numbers, they had prepared for me to be transported to the hospital for a blood transfusion. The doctor asked me to sit tight because he needed to speak with the lead doctors to explain to them what he saw in terms of my state of being. After waiting a while, the nursing assistants came in and they rolled in a table full of medical devices and equipment. I was confused when they asked for permission to hook me up to an IV. I thought they were just going to give me an iron booster, but instead, they were prepping for an emergency blood transfusion.

*Be still, and know that I am God.*
—**Psalm 46:10**

Have you ever had a feeling that something just wasn't right? I wasn't trying to be difficult, but something just did not sit right with me with this plan. At this point, I felt uneasy about going through the process. I refused to accept the suggested emergency blood transfusion and the hospital transport. They pulled the doctor immediately and he came in to discuss his consultation with the lead doctors.

The doctor basically said that my numbers were in the range of someone who is comatose. He apologized and stated that he was not authorized to release me. The lead doctors were concerned and understandably so, because that's what the textbook says. They advised me to prepare for the blood transfusion, but still, something just did not sit right with me. I would have felt much more comfortable if my primary doctor was available to review my results. The doctor gave me a look of concern. I then asked him if my refusing the emergency procedure would kill me that night. I wanted to wait until the next morning so that my primary doctor could review my results. He responded that he couldn't promise that I'd live or die but strongly recommended that I get the transfusion right then.

The doctor looked me directly in my eyes and emphasized how critically low my numbers are. He said, "Your numbers are very, very, very low and I've already explained to you how your condition should be of comatose, but I can't hold you against your will. You look fine, all of your vitals are fine, and I'm basically baffled because this does not match what we learned in medical school. This is not the protocol, it goes against everything that we learned."

Honestly, I don't think my numbers had ever been as low, but they had been close. Still didn't feel right. The doctor went to get the paperwork because I was signing myself out against his recommendations. He was a cool doctor. He talked me through everything and assisted me with making an early appointment with my doctor. As we signed the documents, he looked at me again. He said, "I can tell you don't smoke. I can tell you don't drink. I can tell you exercise. Those things saved your life. Otherwise, you would've been out cold way before your number even got to this point." He then motioned his hand over his head and stated, "You are covered."

I responded, "Absolutely and Amen!"

The staff could not understand how I was walking, talking, and thinking coherently. They said they were amazed and it was as if I were a bionic woman. I don't know about me being a bionic woman but for sure my father is a bionic man! Regardless of what the textbook says or what the doctors say, God has the final say.

The next day I went to my primary doctor, who went through my information and confirmed that my numbers were lower than ever before. When you get blood work done, you receive about thirty numbers in the results. Mine revealed three critically low numbers associated with my red blood cells, but others such as blood pressure and oxygen level checked out fine.

My doctor changed me to a different iron pill and instructed me to continue taking three a day. I scheduled to return for testing. Leading up to that next appointment, family and friends asked me how I was feeling and sent me wishes for a speedy recovery. But in honesty, I often forgot about my health scare because I never felt any symptoms. The only bad thing that came out of it was that I had to cancel my trip to Italy—good thing I purchased travel insurance!

Two weeks later, my numbers rose to a level that I had not seen in almost twelve years. With such an improvement in my numbers, my doctor reduced the number of pills required from three a day to two a day. A few months after, the results showed that I was no longer anemic and didn't have to take the pills any longer!

*Daughter, your faith has healed you. Go in peace.*
—Luke 18:42

I thank God for covering me. I thank Him for not allowing me pass out. I thank Him that I didn't slip into a coma. I thank Him that I didn't have to have an unnecessary blood transfusion.

Now, I start and end my day in prayer and in thanks:

*Father God, I thank You for waking me up to see another day. I know that You didn't have to do it, but I am so grateful that You did. Please forgive me for all of my sins and for all the ways that I fall short of will. In Jesus' name, I ask You to lead me and guide me to those things that are in Your will. Remove any thought, desire and/or action from me that is not is accordance to Your will. Empty me out and fill me up with You. May every person that I come in contact with see none of me, but all of You.*

*Continue to allow me to be a vessel for You. Continue to allow me to glorify Your name. Continue to allow me to carry out the purpose that You have placed upon my life. Please cover me and shield me from negativity anything that will tempt or keep me from carrying out Your will. In all things, I will continue to give You all of the honor and all of the praise. Amen!*

# A Spiritual Recess

## MARIAN CURRIE

I grew up as the oldest girl in a family of seven boys and five girls. I held most of the responsibility in taking care of household chores. I was the self-proclaimed second mom when my parents were not at home, but when giving out orders for chores to my younger siblings, they vehemently reminded me that I was not their mother. Much of the time I had to put my hands on their butts to remind them just who I was. After all, I was the big sister, always there to help take care of everyone's needs.

I spent what seemed like all of my young life taking care of others and letting them depend on me. When I wasn't cooking and cleaning, I was doing hair or playing with my younger siblings. I loved being a part of a large family. We were very close and always had lots of fun. But the pressure and responsibility of being the oldest girl in a large family was overwhelming. While I very much wanted to please my parents, I often felt frustrated because I wanted to play and be carefree like the others. I had too much expected of me.

My solution was to take small breaks from my chores and the daily routine. Whether it was sitting on the back porch steps or down by the little brook that flowed in the woods below our house, I treasured the quietness and my thoughts with the Lord. It released the same kind of good endorphin and euphoria that children get from playing tag or jump rope. It may seem like abnormal behavior for a twelve-year-old to go in the woods to pray, but this was my playtime, what I called a spiritual recess.

Recess comes from the Latin word *recesses*, meaning a going-back, retreat. These spiritual recesses formed some of my most precious inner thoughts and laid the foundation for prayer, which I would use in challenging times to come. I would write poetry or read my little red New Testament Bible. I think this is where I learned to pray and talk to God. I would say, "Lord, are you up there? Do you see what I'm going through? You know my heart and how I feel. You put me here, so help me deal with my mom and dad, and my sisters and brothers."

Have you ever stolen away from your responsibilities to get revived and recharged? Did you feel guilty for doing so? Later in life, I learned that you don't need to feel bad for taking time to be renewed. Taking spiritual recesses interrupts the brain from the cares of life and keeps some of us from going over the edge. I always felt encouraged and uplifted afterwards, like I was recharged to go one more round with whatever I was facing.

One cold November day in 1983, my life was headed in a new and exciting direction in more ways than I could imagine. I felt that the Lord had a plan for my life, and the faith I had in Him and myself had me looking forward to the adventures ahead. My father took me to the airport, and it was the longest twenty minutes of my life. When we got there, he asked me once more before I boarded the plane, this time with watery eyes, "Are you sure you want to go?"

Yes, sir, I do. But my response was not as strong or certain as that. To leave the protection of the most loving father a girl could have was extremely frightening and left me with great feelings of uncertainty. Even still, I knew this was something I had to do. Against my father's own desires to keep me close, he found a distant relative for me to live with, three hundred miles away from our home in North Carolina. I wanted a change and he made it happen.

"Call me when you get there," he said. "I love you."

As I boarded the plan, I looked back and we waved by once more. He was visibly crying this time. I tried to hold back my tears, but it all broke loose once I sat down in my seat. With that, we were in the air. After about thirty minutes, the air inside the plane seemed to get thinner, and all of a sudden, I felt faint. Feelings of fear and loneliness gripped my mind and body as I headed off into the darkness of a new city. This was one of those times for a spiritual recess.

I have learned that, as often as fear, loneliness, or pain return to face us, we must also return to prayer and the foundation that was laid when we first received a breakthrough. It doesn't matter how long ago or at what age, you must go back in your mind and take a spiritual recess. I pulled out my little red New Testament, just like the one I had when I was a child, and began to read the 18th Psalm:

> "I will love You, Oh Lord, my strength. The Lord is my rock and my fortress and my deliverer. My God, my strength, in whom I will trust. My shield and the horn of my salvation, my stronghold. I will call upon the Lord, Who is worthy to be praised, so shall I be saved from my enemies."

And this was my prayer:

*Lord, above all else, You made me and know everything about me. You know my beginning and my end. You brought me here. I know You have a plan for me and will keep me in all my ways. You, Lord, are my protector provider, who promised to give me strength when I am faced with adversity. I believe it. Thank You. In Jesus' name, Amen.*

As the airplane began its descent, I was strengthened and encouraged in my heart and mind. Washington, D.C., was beautiful at night. The lights of the city gleamed in my eyes like a million twinkling stars on a clear summer sky. Butterflies filled my stomach, and my mind was nervous, racing with excitement. We landed, and so my journey and new life began.

After about two years in D.C., I'd found my way around. The little country girl got adjusted to city life. My parents didn't know it at the time, but I had begun living with my boyfriend. My old roommate did not want to continue sharing an apartment, so I had no place else to live. I knew shacking up was wrong and felt guilty, so I went to church and rededicated my life to the Lord. I told my boyfriend that we could no longer sleep together unless we were married, and he reluctantly agreed.

On New Year's Eve in 1985, he forced me to have sex with him. It was horrible. I wanted to leave, but had nowhere to go. When I found out I was pregnant a few months later, his feelings towards me completely changed. He became verbally abusive, and eventually asked me to move out. My world and the dreams I had for myself were shattered. I had never felt more alone or frightened than at that moment.

What would I do? Where would I go? I had no real family or any friends in the area. What would my parents think? I had been raised in a loving, but strict Christian home. My father was a pastor and my mother was an elder. This was not what they expected: their oldest daughter, the strong, big sister to be pregnant out of wedlock. I felt ashamed and embarrassed.

When life presents you with a plan that is different from the one you had envisioned, how do you handle it? How do you catch a curve ball when you don't know it is being thrown? You cannot plan for every twist and turn that life throws your way. Instead, you must somehow go back to the place where you had your first encounter God and grab hold for the strength to press on. If there is any spiritual foundation there, no matter how weak, you will renew your mind and build on from there.

I knew having a baby would change everything. This was the defining moment when I realized that a lifetime of spiritual recesses would be critical for my journey. I went back to the brook in the woods. When I prayed, I cried out like David in Psalms 86. I was comforted and received strength, just as I'm sure David had when he faced his dilemma:

> "Bow down Your ear, O Lord, hear me; for I am poor and needy. Preserve my life, for I am holy; You are my God; Save Your servant who trust in You! Be merciful to me, O Lord, for I cry to you all day long. Rejoice the soul of Your servant, for to You, Oh Lord, I lift up my soul. For you are good, and ready to forgive, and abundant in mercy to all those who call upon you."

In the months and years that followed, spiritual recesses became an everyday way of life for me. As a single parent, you go through many difficulties in which anxiety, fear, loneliness, shame, and more come to meet you. But, through prayer and faith, adjustments can be made that allow your strength and mental fortitude to push you through the challenges on your journey.

In 1998, my career was going well, and I was preparing to complete my college degree. In July of that year, twelve years after having my first son, I found myself pregnant a second time. How could I let this happen again? I never wanted to be that girl, unmarried with two children by two different men. Devastated cannot begin to describe how I felt. I had been living a "Christian" life, abstaining as much as I could from sex and actively attending church. I thought I had mastered the spiritual recesses. Prayer and reading God's word always changed my perspective on situations and things always got better. But this time, I could not see light through my disappointment and fear. I wanted to die.

Pregnant again. The father was still getting himself together. He had asked me to marry him, but for various reasons, I had delayed my answer. In fact, I was about to break it off with him all together before I became pregnant. But how would I raise two children all by myself? It was hard enough with one. Do you sometimes feel as though you have taken a hundred steps forward, only to be thrown back ninety-nine? All of the emotions of guilt, fear, and uncertainty had picked me up and dropped me off at a place of dismal hopelessness. But, I had been at a similar place before. I remembered that things don't always turn out the way we hope for or plan. The Lord tells us in the scriptures, "For I know the thoughts that I think towards you, says the Lord, thoughts of peace and not evil, to give you a future and a hope" (Jeremiah 29:11 NKJV).

Have feelings of hopelessness ever flooded your mind because of a situation you faced? Could a prayer break from reality help you see things differently? At the time, I didn't want to take a spiritual recess from my dark reality; I wanted to relish in the darkness of the pain. It was my punishment, and besides, I felt as though no spiritual recess would bring me hope. But, it did.

The strength came through a trusted friend. Without judgment, she allowed me to cry on her shoulder and prayed with me. Sometimes, you just need a prayer partner to take a spiritual recess with you. I gained encouragement and found the strength to stand up and go on. I had the baby, dropped the boyfriend, and didn't look back. It has been over thirty years since I became a single mom and it hasn't been easy. Countless tears shed, many difficult and challenging times. But, today, I have two beautiful adult children who I raised to be kind and loving human beings.

My mind often returns to my childhood years when I felt that heavy responsibility of being the oldest girl in a large family. As a twelve-year-old, I thought my life was too much to bear. I felt the need to steal time away from the cares of my little life to recharge and renew my mind through prayer and God's word. My spiritual recesses always allowed me to give my burdens and cares over to the Lord. Those spiritual recesses laid a foundation that helped anchor my faith, increase my inner strength, and create an attitude of tenacity necessary to handle all of the challenges I faced as an adult.

How often do you take a spiritual recess? How do you feel afterwards? Do they change how you see things? A spiritual recess is meant to serve as a break in routine, a worthy interruption for prayer that's necessary to revive, renew our minds, and give encouragement and hope. Take them as often as necessary!

## A Spiritual Recess Prayer

Lord, I take this time to break away from the cares of life that weigh me down and to look towards You. You are Supreme. There is nothing that You cannot do. You spoke me into existence, created me in Your image. Therefore, I am powerful, and there is no problem or situation I cannot handle. I walk away from fear, worry, anxiety, hopelessness, insecurity, defeat, fear, and shame. With open arms, I run towards Your wisdom, love, forgiveness, and protection.

Lord, I humble my heart and open my mind to receive from You. Thank You for wisdom and clear direction. Thank You for peace of mind. Thank you for making all things work for my good.

In Jesus' name I pray, Amen.

# Forever in My Heart

RUBY MABRY

My dad was from the beautiful island of Haiti. He was a model in his younger years. He later went to college in Kingston, Jamaica to study the culinary arts. He became a chef. He met my mother on the bus by accidentally stepping on her foot; from then, he began courting her. Back in those times, he had to have permission from her parents to date her, so most of their dates were in her parents' home. He always said it was love at first sight.

He married my mother in 1964. They migrated to the United States and moved to New York. They later had four kids in Brooklyn. My dad was the head chef at the local hospital for over twenty years. He loved to cook, give back, and make people laugh. My parents became United States citizens in 1979 after ten years. It was a monumental moment for them—they were so proud when they were sworn in at the courthouse.

My dad was a great husband, father, provider, teacher, disciplinarian, chef, and comedian. He was well liked by all he came in contact with. He taught me how to dance, cook, be fashionable, have respect for myself, and be a lady. One of my fondest memories was when he did our hair. It was a chance to talk about things that were going on, boys, being a woman, and life in general. He was a compassionate soul who always had a smile on his face.

On top of being a role model and friend, my dad worked hard to make sure we always had food to eat, clothes on our backs, shelter, and all the best that he could provide for his family. He financially provided for eight people: his wife, four of his kids, and two additional kids, his niece and nephew. And he kept us busy: we had piano lessons, participated in Pathfinders (like Boy and Girl Scouts), sang in the choir, attended private school—basically, anything to keep us focused, positively distracted, and more well-rounded. We did not have it all, but we had more than most: we had the love that most children yearn for, which surpasses material items any day.

My parents were well known in our community for being good Samaritans. I always say we had a hotel growing up because my parents would take people in, help them get on their feet, and then they would leave. I myself lived at home until a little after high school. After I married, we moved with the military out of state, then out of the country, then back to the States.

Today, I see that my foundation at home is what makes my "why" strong. My family is what I live and work so hard for. Family is the most important thing. I watched my father sacrifice years of his life, only working hard and not getting a chance to fully live his life. But his contentment was providing for his family; just seeing us happy and cared for was enough for him. Thanks to his, I was able to work on myself and excel in all that I put my mind to. I did not want to live to an old age and not use the gifts that I was born with.

While I was in Michigan, on June 10, 1994, my dad was in a car accident. The car hit him on the driver side and his chest plowed into the steering wheel. He was found to have a cardiac/chest contusion and he broke his right wrist. He was kept overnight for observation and released the next day. I returned home to Florida and assisted with his care and appointments. He began undergoing physical therapy, and saw orthopedics, chiropractors, and trauma surgeons since he now had chronic lower back pain, and continuously complained of right-sided chest wall pain and sternal pain.

The doctors did not order another chest x-ray, despite his incessant cry for help in regards to his chest pain. He eventually had problems breathing in the wee hours of the morning. One night, we called 911 and found out he was having a heart attack. On this second hospital stay, doctors realized that he had the same pulmonary contusion. A tube was inserted into his chest to drain the fluid from his lungs. We stayed at the hospital all day and, during that time, dad seemed to know it was all coming to an end. He told us about his insurance policy and how he felt sick and frustrated over this whole situation. He felt this could have all been avoided had he gotten proper care the first time he was hospitalized.

Later that evening, I kissed him good night on the forehead, making the smooching sound repetitively as he always did for me, and told him that we would see him tomorrow. My younger brother went the next morning to the hospital to shave our dad and help clean him up, but the nurses would not let him into the room. They said they were having a problem. Ironically, a few minutes before all of this happened, my father called the house. A nurse must have dialed the numbers for him. My father asked us when we were coming to the hospital and if we knew where he was. He seemed so tired. We told him we were on our way and would see him soon.

Soon after that, my dad had cardiopulmonary arrest. When we arrived, we were stopped by the social worker. My younger brother told us that there were about ten people in the room working on him. He was transferred to the critical care unit and put on an artificial respirator. He could not have any visitors except for family. What occurred was that the chest contusion from his car accident had developed into a pulmonary (lung) abscess, which ruptured into the pleural space. This resulted in sepsis.

He stayed in the hospital a few days. The doctors declared him brain dead and stated that there was nothing they could do for him. The family had to make a decision to either keep him there, unresponsive, or to take him off the assistive machines. We prayed, prayed, and prayed again. The chaplain prayed with us. Family and friends prayed with us. We called for his brothers and sisters who lived out of state.

My father had always stated that he did not want to be on life support or to stay alive with the aid of machines. After much prayer and deliberation, we all agreed to remove the machines and signed the paperwork. I watched from afar as my mother sat in her wheelchair in total disbelief and shock. She was frail and helpless, not understanding how this could be happening.

My father passed away two days later. A few days after that, we had the funeral. This was one of the toughest days of my life. He was buried on his wedding anniversary. He always told us that, if he should ever pass, he did not want to be "kept on ice" for too long and that he wanted to have a speedy funeral, regardless of who could make it or not.

I was in total disarray. I saw him lying there, looking like someone else, nothing like the strong man who raised me. His makeup was chalky and gray. His lips were too pink. I was numb. My mother was beside herself, also numb, just looking at the casket. I gritted my teeth and had to be so strong so she could remain stronger. I've heard that good people always leave too soon, but I couldn't believe this was happening to our family. He was our backbone.

It was the final time for farewells before the casket was closed. I walked up and felt like my feet were lead. I bent over and kissed his stiff lips, whispered goodbye, and told him I loved him. I then came to an enormous realization: I was now fatherless. I was now forced to grow up and take care of my mother.

I felt so alone, and in the weeks to come, I asked, "Why me? God, why?" I prayed for answers. The first prayer I went to was Isaiah 41:10: "Don't be afraid for I am with you. Don't be discouraged, for I am your God. I will strengthen you and help you. I will hold you up with my victorious right hand." The words, "Don't be afraid for I am with you," gave me strength. It made me feel that, even though I felt lost, God was always with me. He had my back. I felt sad, but strong and supported. The words "I will strengthen you and help you" also replayed in my mind heavily. It helped me through my grieving and reminded me that God does not give us more than we can bear. Needless to say, my faith intensified during this tragic period of time. I prayed, I fasted, and I sang. I was made an even stronger woman and was brought closer to God, which was what my family needed and what I needed. God reminded us that, even though our father was gone, he would always with us in spirit, watching over us and protecting us.

I had to be strong and get out of my negative mindset and self-pity, and take over where my father left off. He was counting on me. His life definitely impacted me and the world in a positive way. He will never be forgotten and he will forever be in my heart.

I also soon came to learn that we are truly just passing through and nothing in life lasts forever. We must cherish the moments we have with our loved ones and value the relationships and time we have with them. A parent is the foundation of a child and, when that parent leaves, the child can feel lost and hopeless. If you experience such a loss, make sure you have someone to talk to and something to do like a new hobby, exercise, meditation, music, or journaling to help you though the tough times. And of course, pray.

My wish in sharing this story is to bring hope, faith, and a mindset shift. Life is short and nothing is guaranteed. Use all of your gifts and share them with the world. Keep God first in all that you do—if you live your life with integrity and you work hard, good things are bound to happen to you. We must all go through losses in our lives whether we want to or not. So do not let them dictate the outcome. Out of my pain, my "why," my father and family, became much more detailed and meaningful. My "why" helped me to keep pushing when I wanted to give up.

Remember to live your life abundantly each day. Continue to feed your soul with positivity and know that faith moves mountains. God is always the plug.

# Death Brought Me Life

## MILTON DICKERSON

Throughout my life, I experienced death from afar. You know, the cliché: "I'm so sorry for your loss" or "my condolences." Those words would fumble from my lips so easily because death didn't impede my existence. It was a part of what I considered to be life, but not my life. I was convinced that death was a thing that passed just like the sun set and the moon rose. Why boggle myself with something that was so natural?

It was not until a string of deaths directly impacted me that I realized that death does have a sting, just as Jesus proclaimed, "O, death where is thy sting?" A sting that's everlasting. A sting that wasn't talked about by those same people that I thought I had comforted with my shower of words and thoughts. A sting that is so lasting that it causes you to question your being, the existence of life, and God. Soon, death became the most pressing thing on my mind. I began to feel it and it seemed to creep up on me. I found myself in a dark place and everything around me started to cave in.

But, death's sting on me was just like the bee in the spring, a sensation that fades away over time. Time does bear a place in the healing process, but it was through prayer and reflection that I truly understood that death *is* a part of life. I had to find a means of coping with death just as I enjoyed living. Am I suggesting I to enjoy death? No, but death does have purpose and that purpose is beautiful.

Death is an expression of life's order. It has a place, just as barriers and challenges do. Anything that separates you from your ultimate happiness can be classified as a barrier. At one point in my life, prison, moving out, and failed communications created barriers for me or stopped my progress. We often overlook the richness in our lives because we become overwhelmed with the barriers that impede our progress. However such challenges serve two purposes: to reveal what needs to be worked on or to test and measure your growth.

Let us begin with revelation, the act of something being revealed or shown. First, revelations come from experience and are not always clear. I had to experience a lot in order to actually see the purpose of death, which now leads me to write this chapter. Like the old saying, "Hot, Hot," I grew up tapping on cold stoves to ensure that it was safe for me to touch. But one must always experience and seek understanding in order to see a purpose in anything. I'm not saying that there is a formula, but I did pray on the act of death to gain a clear vision.

Now, let us examine death as a measurement of growth. Through death, I learned that things often happen in cycles or a pattern and you learn what's next. If you look closely, things can become predictable and be calculated. For example, I recall failing one of my only classes when I was still in school. My mama didn't play that, but by this time, I was in college and was distraught knowing that I was not going to be successful.

Then, during a weekly check-in with my grandfather, we discussed "happenings" in our lives. He was aware that I was struggling in this class. In fact, on a latest test, I had just scored a C. When I began to express myself and denounce my progression, my Pop-Pop stopped me and asked a simple but profound question, "Did you learn anything?" When I replied, "Yes, sir," he immediately proclaimed, "Well, it wasn't a waste of time!" From this, I learned that life is all about reflecting on one's growth and how you measure up to yourself. The same can be said about death and adversity: they force you to reflect. Look in the mirror and develop who you are.

I will now explore how death impeded me and how I overcame its sting through reflection. When the tragedies hit, I was in the prime of my career, in graduate school, and beginning to write. Out of nowhere I was slammed with the fact that one of my aunts and a cousin had passed away. I collapsed to the floor in disbelief that they were gone. I began to question the existence of God. How could a Creator destroy His creation? I swelled in tears and pain. I suffocated in knowing that life as I knew it was now changed forever.

Although, they passed at separate times, I experienced my aunt's and my cousin's deaths together. They both contributed so much to me and so specifically that a piece of me left with them, or so I thought. The barrier of death impeded my life to the point that I began to swim in despair and, by the time I realized, I landed far away from reality and lost sight of the purpose of death. How can one gain anything from something that brings about so much pain?

Still, I could not remain down. First, I had to understand that, with his or her death, each individual's contributions to earth had expired. They spent their time sowing seeds in me and other people. Now that the tears have dried, I see that the sting of death leaves warm and loving impressions of those individuals on the living. There was plenty that I could learn from both of them and that I could live up to even though they were now gone. It was because of their touch.

My aunt was a gel that bonded my family together. She enjoyed traveling and seeing her family. She also prayed for the well-being of all, was caring and compassionate, and made sure that her dozens of nieces and nephews all felt special. On the other hand, my cousin was a cheerleader, a musician, a lover of music, and a supporter. She captured an audience like no other and was loved in her community.

These two individuals both provided gems that I now hold on to as I progress. Their deaths represented a revelation for me: in their passing, they imparted a well of riches for my life to come. Although I initially treated their deaths as barriers to my happiness, now I understand that death can bring life.

The deaths of my grandfather, godfather, and pastor represented tests of my growth (or the lack thereof). A few years after the deaths of my aunt and cousin, I started to feel again and began completing things I had left undone. My godfather marked the first of the trio, his death landing me in a familiar nowhere. I was lost again, but this time, I went numb. I went through the motion of fielding calls and hearing the memories of old times, once again, neglecting to mourn and celebrate his life properly.

You see, my godfather represents the earthly being of who I am: the go-getter, the talker, the thinker, the overall good guy. I watched him move and he showed me things that I otherwise would have never known. For example, when I landed my first teaching job, I wanted to purchase a new car and he told me very specifically not to purchase a brand new car. He said, "Get established, then get a car." It went in one ear and out the other, and I brought the car.

When I lost the car soon after, he asked me to go out of town with him and his wife. Mind you, the trip was supposed to be in this car I lost. He started the conversation out with, "Well, I'm gonna address the elephant in the room. Didn't I tell ya not to get the car?" His wife, with grace, called his name to stop him, but he replied, "I need to share manhood with him." Yes, he did scold me, but more importantly, he taught me how to plan and execute my plan from that day forward. After his death, I came to cherish these lessons he'd taught me even more and was able to move forward to honor his life.

Just as my godfather had, my pastor also planted many seeds in my life. He taught me to be an avid reader and to study not only the Word, but also life. He taught me how to interpret many concepts and to explain them in a way that was simple enough for a child to understand; furthermore, he helped me apply and execute principles in my life. At his passing, I was jarred. But this time, I kept on going, because I knew the purpose of his passing.

Lastly, my grandfather: the comedian, the life of the party, the crowd mover, the listener. I can write a whole other chapter describing his gifts bequeathed to me. I cannot even begin to express how his life, and death, changed me. But at this point, I knew that death is truly life: like I learned in science, no matter can ever be destroyed, only transferred. And when I turned to the Word of God, He proclaimed the same thing. In fact, all my life, I had been taught to cope with death through the most powerful death of them all: the crucifixion and resurrection of Jesus.

The Spirit drew my attention further to the fact that a seed and its blossom can't exist at the same time. In order for those peoples' legacies to continue on, what was planted must die and transform to life. I grew to understand that death is a beginning to an end. It completes a cycle. The oxymoron of death allowed me to live my life to the fullest through death. Yes, *through death,* I can live my life. Death goes beyond a physical expression. No, this transition is not easy, but it is a brighter view to the state of being.

I challenge you to substitute barriers with life. As I pen this work, I reflect on my progress and ask myself, "How did I overcome some of those barriers?" Mostly in isolation—I smiled when everyone was looking, but deep down inside, I was torn up. However, death taught me to express those emotions as often as I could. Talking about them helped water those seeds that were planted and caused them to live, allowed for the memories and lessons to resurrect in me. I may now continue the cycle, so that I can show others what I have learned.

I soon began to take care of that sting of death. Put ointment on it and even a Band-Aid, which reminded me that the sting would only be temporary. I did this by traveling throughout my healing process, finding things that made me happy, and purposing those things in my life. Meanwhile, I connected and reconnected with people who I had cut off in my dark period. I apologized and re-forged my friendship with them to continue making more memories.

I recall being stung by a bee only a few times in my life; now, I try to avoid them at all costs because of the everlasting impression they made. I will never see my cousin on a stage again or receive my grandfather's attention, but I do know it's inevitable that one will get stung. Death will come. But I remind you now that there is power in the sting of death—therein lies life. Live your life knowing that you are improving.

# Forgive! Live Through It, Grow Through It

REV. ALLISON G. DANIELS

When a very dear best friend of over fifteen years betrayed me, it truly hurt me to the core of my heart. This was the one person who I could count on through thick and thin. We laughed together, sang together, ate together, and worked together. I knew in my heart that I would have to one day forgive her, forget, and move on with my life. But every time I tried to look on the bright side of things, I really wasn't sure that I could do it on my own. It was bigger than Allison.

I thought about Jesus' journey and how He said to his Father, "Father, forgive them, for they know not what they do." But I wasn't Jesus. I thought about Joseph when he forgave his brothers for selling him into slavery out of jealousy, and then lying to their father and saying that Joseph was dead. But again, I wasn't Joseph.

I couldn't forgive my best friend no matter how hard I tried, and honestly, I didn't want to forgive her. That was the last thing on my mind. I found out through a third party at work—not through my best friend—that she was having an affair with the man I had planned to marry. Of course, this took me by surprise. I was in total disbelief because she was always together with me and my fiancé, whether it was the three of us going out to dinner, to the movies, or to lunch.

In so many ways, I looked out for her—I had her back. I had her covered and we even rode to work together because she didn't have a car of her own. However, one morning, I wasn't feeling well so I had my fiancé drop her off on his day off and he later dropped me off at work around 10:30 am. It was a Thursday morning.

When I arrived to work mid-day, I walked into my office kitchen and unexpectedly overheard another coworker say to my best friend, "Does Allison not know that you've been sleeping with her fiancé for over two years? She's still going to marry him?" I stopped in my tracks, stuck. For several months, my coworkers had been repeatedly throwing hints and making innuendo comments concerning "someone's" relationship, but I had always laughed it off, not realizing that I was the brunt of their jokes.

I stared my friend in her face and she jumped up out of her chair screaming, "I'm sorry! I'm sorry!" However, her words only pierced deep inside my soul and I felt stunned with pain, anger, and hurt. Although we remained in contact and talked about it on several occasions, things between us were never the same. Yes, I told her that I forgave her, but for a long time whenever I would see her at work, I'd still feel the sting of hurt all over again. So, I knew I was still clinging to some form of resentment and bitterness deep in my heart. I was constantly depressed, lonely, scared, and overwhelmed by this lingering pain, and before I knew it, over five years had passed.

I realized then that, if the healing process was to begin in my life, the first step was to disallow the situation to take control of my head. There were questions I'd ask myself, *What did I do wrong? What had I missed? How could I be so naïve? Did he really love me? Was she really my friend? Why did this happen to me? Did I previously hurt someone along the way and forgot about it? Where is my God in my moment of pain and shame?*

One night, I received a phone call from my friend. She was crying out, "Please, please, Allison, come to the hospital and pray for my father. He has just been admitted into hospice and the doctors do not expect him to live through the night." Immediately, I thought to myself, "How could I, in good conscious, come and pray for someone who she loves, knowing what she did to me? What about the hurt, pain, and agony I went through? The lonely nights waking up in tears, falling off to sleep in tears, jumping up in the middle of the night with panic attacks, the depression and days when I could not eat?"

That was when I realized that I needed a closer, more intimate relationship with God, because I was not going to get through this process by trying to fake my way through. I guess you can say I encountered a "Damascus Road" experience, like the Apostle Paul. And I needed it: the laughter at work was continuing and, amidst their snickering, their smiles, and my own bitter responses towards them, I needed to hear God's voice. I needed to pray myself through a healing journey and get off this rollercoaster ride that I was on.

Every night, I read my Bible and said this prayer:

## A Prayer for Healing and Forgiveness

*Dear God, I come boldly before Your throne, acknowledging that You are the Most High God. You sit high and You look low. You are all wise and all knowing. You are my redeemer, my shield and buckler, my bright morning star and most gracious Lord. You are the Prince of Peace.*

*I acknowledge that I have behaved in a manner that was not pleasing in Your sight. I have harbored the spirit of unforgiveness in my heart and I need You to show me how to make things right with my dear friend. So I ask for Your forgiveness and I seek forgiveness for my dear friend. You are a God of peace and restoration and I thank You now for restoring my relationship with my dear friend. In Jesus' Name, Amen!*

Just as it is written in Romans 10:8-13, I believed in my heart and I confessed with my mouth His Lordship over me. I also repented and confessed my wrong doing in the relationship. I realized that I have the right to come to Him, thank Him first for His great plan of salvation, and know that He does all things well and in order.

As I developed a consistent prayer, I soon came to accept God's forgiveness and her forgiveness. And by forgiving my friend, I built the strength I needed, through Jesus, to live, love, and laugh again. More importantly, I am now a better Christian who has matured in the Lord, because I am able to get along with others who might act differently than me. Instead of getting angry, I express myself and my concerns towards others in a tactful and compassionate manner. Nobody is perfect! I simply let go and let God, and remain confident that His Word will continually strengthen me. In fact, His Word tells me to seek first His kingdom and His righteousness, and all the blessings will be added unto me.

My friend and I have now made amends and we are still in touch. She is now married and raising a family herself, and still calls me her best friend. I have most definitely forgiven her and have forgiven myself as well!

Surrender your all to God. Remember that healing takes time and it's a daily process. No matter what we go through in life, we must learn to live through it and grow through it in the process of healing. God's Word says, "My brethren, count it all joy when ye fall into divers temptations: Knowing this, that the trying of your faith worketh patience. But let patience have her perfect work, that ye may be perfect and entire, wanting nothing" (James 1:2-4 KJV).

Here are some questions to ask yourself during your healing process:

- What does forgiveness mean to you?

- What does healing mean to you?

- Have you talked with the offending person and have they accepted their responsibility?

- Is the relationship you have with this person worth you forgiving them?

- Have you given yourself the proper time to heal?

- Can you see the bigger picture after the healing process?

- Where will these thoughts eventually lead you in the end?

- Are these thoughts and emotions spiritually sound?

- Are these thoughts going to build you up or tear you down?

- Can you share these thoughts with someone without experiencing the hurt all over again?

I believe that God wanted to get me to the point in my life where I can handle things and not flip out or lose my mind. He wanted to get me to a place where I trust Him and not man. Now, I believe that there is beauty in my brokenness and I am embracing my inner emotions and allowing God to take control because I long to see the presence of His goodness in my life. I do not want to be in bondage to the spirit of unforgiveness, so I continue to seek God daily for a renewal of my heart, mind, and body. I've asked Him to restore to me double-fold the things that I lost along the way. He will continue to transform me by showing me how to walk in my authority and unleash the divine power that He has placed inside of me. I will stop living in doubt, fear, and sadness because, in addition to being toxic, they are not of God.

Each day, I encourage you to unload your emotional baggage and step out of your comfort zone. Allow God to heal you from the inside out so that you can get rid of your defeated and unwelcoming attitude. Create your own destiny as to how you want to live your life and be quick to accept and adapt to a positive change. Learn how to develop an intimate relationship with God by fasting and praying yourself through it all. Meditate on these scriptures:

- *Matthew 6:33:* "But seek ye first the kingdom of God, and his righteousness; and all these things shall be added unto you."

- ***Matthew 4:4:*** *"But he answered and said, It is written, Man shall not live by bread alone, but by every word that proceedeth out of the mouth of God."*

- ***Ephesians 4:32***: *"And be ye kind one to another, tenderhearted, forgiving one another, even as God for Christ's sake hath forgiven you."*

In addition, here are other helpful suggestions for the process of forgiving:

- Develop a consistent prayer life.

- Daily read scriptures on healing.

- Write in your journal everyday.

- Write your daily affirmations.

- Change your mindset and focus on positive thoughts.

Claim your acceptance and remember that you are a survivor and an overcomer. You will be able to trust and believe again because everyone you meet is not out to hurt you. You are an overcomer when you stop allowing hurts to become personal. Learn self-love and be at peace with yourself. Allow the healing process to begin with you, and you will be free.

## A Prayer of Affirmation
*(Live Through It, Grow Through It)*

*Father God, I welcome You to reign in my life and in all my situations. I bind the hands of the enemy and cancel every assignment that the enemy has over me. Lord God, I believe that I shall live and not die and that I will see Your goodness and Your favor in my life. I believe Your Word that no weapon formed against me shall prosper.*

*Father, I take authority over the spirit of confusion and denounce it in the Name of Jesus. I command any spirit that is not in line with Your Word to not prosper in my life. God, I know that You have me covered and that You will not let the cares of this world overwhelm me or take me off my focus. You are with me and You will never leave me nor forsake me. I will not compromise for the things that this life offers but I will continue to pursue the plans and purposes that You have for my life. So, Lord, teach me how to live through it, grow through it, shine through it, and love through it. In Jesus' Name, Amen!*

# The Fallout of Prayer

## ROZ KNIGHTEN-WARFIELD

*For I know the plans I have for you, says the Lord.
They are plans for good and not for disaster, to give you a
future and a hope. In those days when you pray,
I will listen. If you look for me in earnest, you will find me
when you seek me. I will be found, says the Lord.
I will end your captivity and restore your fortunes.
I will gather you out of the nations where I sent you and
bring you home again to your own land.*

—Jeremiah 29:11-14 NLT

## Prayer is a Sonic Boom

Many people are not comfortable with prayer. But if I'm ever asked or invited to a prayer gathering, yes, you will find me in the front row. I am passionate about it and want to share my journey of prayer, praise, and worship.

I think of prayer as a sonic boom: whether done individually or communally, it creates a supernatural transformation that transcend through the air faster than the speed sound. The power of prayer is a spiritual megaphone that amplifies a daily communication of sound. Why do I so embrace the power of prayer? Because I trust in the Lord. The teachings of Jeremiah 29:11-14, who was known as the weeping prophet, reminds us to not fear the future and displays hope in a chaotic era such as our current season of the 21$^{st}$ century.

I was raised up with the practices of prayer. Morning, afternoon, and evening, I saw my mommie's Bible open with fresh markings. I often peeked in through her bedroom door and saw her praying and chatting with the Father as though He were sitting on the edge of her bed. Even though I had not yet embraced the treasure of prayer, it has always been clear that it was a form of relational currency with whom I call today the Original Big Daddy of My Life. Yes, I'm talking about Abba, also known as Jehovah, the Great Father, and a plethora of other names.

My mother taught me to pray often and memorize certain prayers. She gifted me with my first Bible at age twelve and I locked myself in my room most of the summer, eager to read God's Word! The first prayer Mommie taught me was the Lord's Prayer, Matthew 6:9-13 KJV (feel free to memorize any version that is pleasing and meaningful to you).

## The Lord's Prayer

*Our Father which are in heaven, Hallowed by thy name.*

*Thy kingdom come, Thy will be done in earth, as it is in heaven.*

*Give us this day our daily bread.*

*And forgive us our debts, as we forgive our debtors.*

*And lead us not into temptation, but deliver us from evil: For thine is the kingdom, and the power, and the glory, forever Amen.*

Mommie and Grannie explained that the Lord's Prayer was a learning tool that also had the ability to ward off evil that would try to harm my success. Eventually, I began to pray verbiage of my own will, petitioning for gratitude, forgiveness, and needs. Prayer allowed (and still allows) me to have personal chat sessions all day long with Daddy, much like a child having a conversation with her parent. You don't have to stand in line. He's always a prayer away—just call Him up! You can even set a table for two and have your morning coffee with Him. It's that simple! To those saying, "Girl, it just ain't that easy:" well, it is when you decrease your ego and increase with Daddy.

Mommie said that prayer is everything! That one could ask for guidance, protection, provision, and much more, but that it is mainly for thanksgiving, adoration, and gratitude. When in troubled scenarios, she praised Him instead of asking for an immediate fix, knowing and trusting that Daddy is a sustainer of His promised word. She said that peace would overcome her when she chose to praise the situation instead of being stressed and anxious about trying to tell Daddy what to do. Her focus and praise always displayed that she was not the least worried about her outcome. He had already made provisions. Talk about joy during the trials—if I had not witnessed the countless blessings myself, I wouldn't believe it either.

## Some Tips to Craft Your New Prayer Lifestyle

Philippians 4:6-7 NLT tell us not to worry about anything, but to pray about everything. Tell God what you need, and thank Him for all he has done. If you do this, you will experience God's peace, which is far more wonderful than the human mind can understand. His peace will guard your hearts and minds as you live in Christ Jesus.

As I studied the word of God, I formulated my very own prayer life. Lo and behold, daily practices were turning into a lifestyle of prayer that I had always witnessed in Mommie and Grannie. I was in a love affair with God's word. Life seemed a lot easier when I mediated on prayer, day and night. The frustrations of life were no longer causing distractions.

Now, I want you to think about all the many skill sets you have learned in life. Remember the reading, research, resources, practices, and timing you had to put in to become a champion of that particular skill set. Prayer requires the same endurance! With that I'd like to introduce to you to six tips to develop a consistent prayer life that looks uniquely like you!

1. **Build an intimate relationship with your Bible.** We first must learn and engage with God's word every day. If this has not been a regular practice for you, it's okay to take baby steps. In no time, you will have a yearning passion to know more about God. Make the word of God your BOO (Beloved Only One) and have a love affair with your Bible. It's promised to be the only permissible affair God will honor.

2. **Commit to yes!** Be committed to your "yes" to create a thriving prayer life that will be a refreshing spring of water and rejuvenation for your soul. I am continuously building my muscles of consistency and endurance, so I too am responsible for my "yes." Let's commit together! Be accountable to yourself, God, and your crew of ego, rational self, and born-again self. Work as a team and transfer power from your ego to your new spiritual self.

3. **Gather up words of empowerment.** Store up your arsenal of words. These are words of empowerment that will affirm that you are more than a conqueror. You can do anything through Christ Who strengthens you. So

get your journal and 3x5 cards ready to memorize God's words, prayers, and scriptures.

4. **Embrace praying for yourself first.** Look in the mirror daily, hug yourself, and repeat, "I, your name here, Simply Make Intentional Love Encounters ™, starting with myself first, then fellow man, then the world." If you have had the opportunity to fly, you know the directions: put the oxygen mask on yourself first, then assist the person next to you! Interesting how God communicates with you!

5. **Believe that Daddy loves you—end of discussion.** This is the whopper. Daddy has unconditional love for you; in fact, He gave up the life of His only begotten son so that you may have everlasting life. Thank goodness for the Father's love lenses and not man's eye of judgment, selfishness, and comparison. God be all Glory, forever and ever.

6. **Go deep in praise and worship daily.** Praise is when you go all out in tribute and applaud all Daddy has done for you. The good, the bad, and the ugly. Speak and shout out loud, be bold about the Father's love. Don't be ashamed! You can do this in the privacy of your own home: you name the time, room, and body position. Add some tunes and allow the spiritual lyrics to be a download from Big Daddy Himself. Record the moments if you need to reflect on your praise session. Think of it as going scuba diving in worship to find hidden treasures of answers,

gratitude, and guidance. Embrace every opportunity of worship. Give honor where honor is due. Lift up your voice to decree and declare a heart of thanksgiving and adoration for the entirety of what the Father has done for you.

This is how I build a fortified prayer life. These tips become a road map and a template that you can use as a guide to start praying in new ways to communicate with the Father. When you feel anxious, depressed, jealous, tempted, or low on self-worth, then run to your closet or your favorite place and pray. You can even take a walk. I call it my morning strolls with Daddy.

Be creative and make your prayer look like you. As you learn the character and nature of God, you will become more comfortable and fully engaged when it's time for those intimate meetings. Daddy wants you be authentic, committed, and, most of all, open-minded to prayer before you start each new day. As James 1:5-8 NLT states, if you need wisdom—if you want to know what Gods wants you to do—ask Him and He will gladly tell you. He will not resent your asking Him. But when you ask Him, be sure that you really expect Him to answer, for a doubtful mind is as unsettled as a wave of the sea that is driven and tossed by wind. People like that should not expect to receive anything from the Lord. They can't make up their minds. They waver back and forth in everything they do.

In the Bible, Daniel prayed three times a day, which is a good goal to work towards. He also fasted. A short 101 on fasting: don't do it for you, but do it unto God for breakthroughs, blessings, and maturity that will catapult you to another level. In addition, remember to study, read, research, and build your library of resources. And while your private prayer time with Daddy is key, always keep contact with a support team who has your best interest at heart. Be willing to share your game plan so that you may be refreshed and you may refresh those who may have grown stale in there prayer time.

Trust me, but more importantly, trust God. Reading your Bible and making a commitment will formulate a flourishing prayer life that will help you be bolder, wiser, more confident, and free to reign in authority of Father's love. Journal or record your journey and be amazed by your growth.

I'll end here: for more resources, look up Tom Dooley, one of my favorite narrators. His ministry is a great supplement when you need some company in your private moments with Daddy. Brother Tom brought glory to the Father through his love for media and he is known for being the world's most fluent narrator. Also, go here: www.oneyearbibleonline.com/nltaudio. This link will parse out the Bible in one year with Old Testament, New Testament, Psalms, and Proverbs. I pray you find joy, ease, and comfort following along, listening and marking your version of the New Living Translation. With Mommie's steadfastness, grannie's motivation to reach a hundred years of age, Brother Tom Dooley's fluency, and the Bible, I'm fully equipped for daily prayer.

Daddy set me up nice real. Thanking Him and praying for myself taught me to love myself as God loves me and not to put condemnation on myself. I don't compare and I'm a designer best, one of a kind.

You too are a designer best, one of a kind! There is no one-size-fits-all with God. Start engaging your Father in daily word study and, before you know it, you will be praying for yourself and others. You are a unique soul and your thumbprint is only yours, nobody else's.

## Prayer of Appreciation

*Daddy, thank You for telling me that I am Your God Priority System and that I can do anything in life because You are my wise counsel. Amen.*

# A Daughter's Prayer from Fear to Faith

TINA MAYO-HUNTER

As a little girl, I lived in fear of losing my mother at a young age. I used to pray to God, "Never to take my mother away from me." I had been through so much with her. All I wanted was for her to get a chance to live a happy life and not have to struggle and worry anymore. The thought always came to mind that, if anything were to happen to my mom, life would be over for me.

My mother was an awesome woman, mother, and friend, and she loved her kids. The only ugly thing about her was that she was addicted to drugs. She had an addictive personality. Why? Because she never took the time to deal with the trials and tribulations in her life and thought drugs would ease the pain. As a kid, I never wanted to leave my mother's side. Although I didn't understand what was going on, I knew she was in some type of pain and needed comfort. I always said this one prayer: "Dear God, please bless my mother and her finances. Take away any pain that she is feeling and give her happiness for the rest of her life."

God heard me. As time went on, my sibling and I grew up and started raising our own families. Despite her condition, my mother always gave her children tough love and showed us how to get out on our own and make good lives for our families. She also eventually decided to turn her life around and give up drugs for good.

I knew God was preparing me for a new journey in my life when I turned my life over to Him in 2011. I made a commitment that I would continue to do the right things in life and live more like Him and not of the world. My mindset started changing: I started praying more, ministering to friends and family, and most of all, I started letting go of all the bad habits. But I didn't realize that I still had a lot of old feelings bottled up in me.

In 2015, I started telling my story little by little about having an addict as a mother. Have you ever held in something for so long that you forgot it was there? Well, that's how I felt. My childhood situation rested heavy on my heart and had also stopped me from doing a lot of things in my life. Fear held me captured, but I didn't know it until I got closer to God and He started revealing specific fears and the reasons for them: why I was afraid to cross bridges, why I was afraid of heights, and why I was afraid to be closed in small spaces. My whole life,

I'd just thought I was being weird about my phobias and that there was something wrong me. And there was something wrong... I needed to let go and let God!

Crossing bridges was one of my greatest struggles. At one point in my life, I would've driven an extra hour to get to my destination than cross over the Woodrow Wilson Bridge. After turning my life over to God and being baptized, I started asking myself, "Why are you still afraid to do the things you asked God to free you from?" So little by little, I started challenging myself by praying and asking God to help me get through what I needed to get through.

One day, I was going to Washington, D.C., and decided I wasn't going to take the long route: I was going to take the Woodrow Wilson Bridge and I did. I had an anxiety attack as soon as I approached the bridge. I grabbed the stirring wheel so dang on hard that it stiffened up on me and all I could say was, "Jesus! Jesus! Jesus!" My heart was beating so hard that the person in the car next to me could've heard my heartbeats. Within seconds, things started calming down and I continued across the bridge. I took deep breaths, and finally, I was back to normal. Later, I asked myself, "What was all that for? What were you afraid of?"

I decided then to trust in God and continue challenging myself until this feeling of fear was completely gone. Don't sit in your mess without calling on your higher power. Many times before, I would find myself in a situation and try to deal with it on my own. Not now: I immediately start calling on Jesus and I tell Him about my situation and how much I need Him. Today, I am happy to say that I can cross the Woodrow Wilson Bridge without fear—instead, I cross Woodrow Wilson Bridge with faith.

My life changed on July 2, 2017. My mother called my home to tell us that she was feeling sick and needed immediate help. My God! When my sixteen-year-old told me that nana was on the phone and was incomprehensible, I knew something was wrong. Once again, I felt weighed down by a ton because of fear. That big bad wolf had crept back from the past.

Immediately, I called on Jesus and He answered. He gave me the calmness that I needed to call the ambulance to her home; I stayed on the phone and prayed the entire time while the dispatcher did her part. I asked God, "Please do not let anything happen to my mother while she is alone." He didn't. The paramedics picked her up and transported to Arlington Hospital.

My baby sister, my children, and my granddaughter all made it there within twenty minutes of mom's arrival in the emergency room. It was such a joy to walk into the room and see my mom sitting up and smiling. We all grabbed hands and started praying over her, letting her know everything would be okay. Finally, the doctor came and told the family that she was being transferred up to the ICU, where they would perform the first emergency surgery.

My mother was bleeding internally and had started throwing up blood in her home before reaching the hospital. Her liver was terribly damaged and, even in the emergency room, her body rejected the medications given to her. The emergency surgery was necessary to tie the bleed in her stomach. Afterwards, my mother was heavily sedated so every time we went back to visit her, she was asleep. She would wake up a few times and acknowledge that we were there with her. Fix It, Jesus" was the name of my song during this process.

The night of July 2nd, the doctors came to us just after midnight to explain exactly what was going on with our mother. Then, they told us that she wouldn't make it. For a moment, everything went silent in my ear. After I got my thoughts together and registered what the doctor had said, I immediately opened my mouth and told her, "We are Christians who believe in God and we believe in miracles. To God be the glory." Remember: I let go and was now operating on the faith of God.

My family and I started speaking life. Immediately, the doctor's language also started changing: she said that we could rest assured knowing that they were going to do everything they could to help my mother. As time went on, I decided to call a friend to talk and tell her how hurt I was feeling and that I was scared. My friend reassured me that God specializes in miracles and I agreed, so we prayed together. After I got off the phone, I got on my knees and began having a private conversation with God about mom and how I was feeling. When I finally got up, I felt like I was in a whole new body, swaddled in a calmness that I couldn't explain. A new strength allowed me to take the focus off of myself and onto my baby sister and the others.

After a week of hospitalization, my mother was transferred to Georgetown Hospital so that she could be under the care of a specialist. After she settled in, we all went to visit and she was so happy to see us! She told us that we all were so beautiful and we all had big smiles on our faces. As time went, we thought she was getting better, but soon, we got an intimidating call from her doctors asking us to come in so we could get a full update on her condition and talk about yet another surgery.

My prayers became much stronger. I asked God to take any pain away from mom and to heal her body so that she would be strong enough to have the surgery that she needed. I prayed that same prayer for days, going back and forth to visit my mom. She was sedated and really didn't know we were there, but we still rubbed and kissed her, and her eyes would blink a little.

Finally, we were able to catch her awake. She told us that she wanted something to drink so the nurse gave her ice chips, and she said the funniest thing!

In her baby voice, she said, "Awwww! That tastes so good."

Honestly, we were just happy to hear her speak to us. My mother loved to talk so not hearing her voice had been a bit hard. We kept on praying for His grace, mercy, and healing. I know God was in the midst because it was revealed early on that she wasn't in any pain. Glory to God is all I could keep on my tongue. I ensured my baby sister that mom would be okay and encouraged her to pray as well.

I woke up on a Thursday, feeling blessed. I was getting myself together and heading to work when my sister called. The doctor wanted the family to come to the hospital so that they could give us an update on everything that had happened the night before. I turned around on the 395, called my job to explain what was going on, and headed back home to get my kids so that we could all meet up at the hospital. All I could do in the midst of this was to ask God for His help, guidance, and strength.

At this time, God had revealed something to me but it wasn't clear until we got to the hospital and I walked into the room. I saw my beautiful mother with tubes in her, struggling to breathe. Though she did not look like herself, God was clear at that moment: my mother was at peace. That's all I could hear, even through the loud cries of my baby sister. God kept telling me that our mother was at peace. I heard Him, not through fear, but faith. I leaned over to my Aunt Margo and told her the sacred news. We started praying over my mother and anointing her with oil in the name of Jesus.

Finally, the doctor came in and confirmed that her condition had worsened overnight. Jesus! Jesus! Jesus! They were telling me something I never imagined but I was somehow okay. After spending the day with our mother, we went home. The doctor called several times to let us know that her breath was decreasing and that it would be within hours that she would be transitioning. I was so calm when the doctor called at 2:15 am to tell me that my mother was gone. At that moment, I started thanking God and praising Him for allowing my mother to go peacefully and with His grace. My heart ached but I was so grateful. I knew wholeheartedly in God that my mother was at peace!

I will always choose faith over fear. Never let go of your prayers: it is what saved my life and helped me to overcome my greatest fears. Today, I stand on faith: The Lord is the strength of my life (Psalms 27:1).


Your Fearless Sister,
Tina

# Father-Daughter Relationship

VERONICA HOWARD

As a child, I always wondered about my father: what he looked like, how he smelled, how he walked, how he talked, how he smiled, how he laughed, how life would have been better for a girl had he been around. The last time I'd seen him was when I was about four-years-old, not that I remember him at all. It was strange to miss someone I couldn't even recognize. I used to dream of this father figure picking me up at my grandparents' house where I lived with my grandfather, my uncle, little sister, and mother. I could never see the man's face.

I was always told that a little girl's first love is her father, but I never could experience it. When I was younger, I thought that my life would've been better had my father been present, especially when it came to dealing with little boys who'd lie to me or use me like a trash can top. When other men know you have a father around who is your protector, they tend to bother you less. I wouldn't have gone through so much bullying and disrespect from guys and neighbors.

I had a loving, caring, praying, humble, and God-fearing mother and I did not come from a broken home, but I always felt the void of my father. I hear a lot of woman say, "I have been his/her mother *and* father." I never could agree with that. A mother can only be a mother and a father can only be a father. The mother is there for nourishment, care, and love. The father is there to provide and protect. The two play entirely different but equally important roles. I used to envy my friends who had fathers to step in when guys hurt their feelings or to make their moms happy, which made the whole house happy.

I had no one to run to when in danger or in need of advice. My father could've told me about the thoughts men have in their heads, things that your mother can't help you with. My heart yearned for fatherly love! Actually, more than that, I wanted a dad. A dad loves you unconditionally and is there through sickness and health, the good and the bad. He teaches a girl about true love so that, later in life, she doesn't get caught up with uncaring men who she tries to "change" (we all know this never happens). Yes, things would have definitely been better and more structured had a *dad* been active in my life.

# Facing My Fears While Trusting in God

*I will bless the Lord at all times:*
*his praise should continuously be in my mouth.*
*My soul shall make her boast in the Lord:*
*the humble shall hear thereof, and be glad. O magnify*
*the Lord with me, and let us exalt His name.*

**— Psalms 34:1-4**

It was the winter of 1997. I had just landed my first government job in the United States Department of Justice. I was twenty-seven-years-old, a late bloomer in life. I had become a mother at the age of twenty and had to sit home on public assistance to raise my baby until she got to an age that was safe and comfortable for daycare. At this point, I was bound to the ghetto life. I always worked and tried to do better as a young single mother, but I was tired. Tired of being tired, and tired of drinking beers and smoking weed to try and feel good.

I constantly thought about my father and my life in parallel. I never fully swallowed the pill of growing up without a dad. I never got over the negative feelings that came with having no father, no male guidance, and no security. As I got older and older, life just kept happening over and over again, and the greatest trial was still ahead. I continuously called on God for help, understanding, guidance, patience, and forgiveness through this trial. I asked Him to ease my pain while going through, not knowing what the outcome would be.

It was May 16, 2017. My sister and I took our families to Puerto Rico to celebrate my sister's, grandkids', and daughter's birthdays, which are all in the month of May. We had just arrived in Rio Mar Puerto Rico. We were at the front desk signing in when my phone rang. When I answered the phone, a strong, pastoral voice came through the receiver calling out my name. V-E-R-O-N-I-C-A. I knew right then and there that this was my father.

I was talking to a stranger but I also felt relieved at the same time. We played catch up, asking questions like "How are your brothers? Are they married? Do they have kids?" You know the questions you ask to keep the phone from going quiet and awkward. It felt good and bad: good to know he was still alive, but bad because I was surrounded by questions. Was he going to stay in my life this time? Was he going to disappoint me again?

While we were on the phone, his house phone rang. He said he was going to call me right back since his company calling. Just before he hung up, he told me that he'd mentioned me to his boys (my father's other kids). After learning this, I decided to reach out to these siblings of mine who I'd never met and didn't know if they would ever accept, trust, or love me.

My brother, who was my father's junior, was easy to find on Facebook. I sent him a message telling him that I was his sister and he replied saying that my father had mentioned me to him once before. He really didn't say too much about what was said but he did know about me, so I figured that was a start. He and I talked about his new marriage and his kids, and I told him about my family as well. He lived in Atlanta, Georgia and was studying to be a minister and was in a gospel group. He was pleasant and I was proud of the man he was.

After speaking with him, I then reached out to my youngest sibling. I sent him a message telling him that I was his eldest sister and he also said that my father had mentioned me to him. Again, that was a relief and kind of made it a little easier to talk with him. The conversation went a little like my conversation with the older brother. My younger brother was a professor at an excellent college and was the director of music for the entire band. No kids and still unmarried. He was pleasant just like the other brother. Then, my younger brother asked me if I had ever taken a blood test with my father. I don't know why I was so startled but I was. I never heard that my father had not claimed me. I think my brother knew he had triggered something in me because, after a long pause, he texted me to ask if was I okay. I said, "Yes." I knew I'd be okay because I had already asked God to be with me through this whole ordeal.

When we started talking about music, I realized why I love music so much. All the way from elementary to high school, I loved the band and played the clarinet and saxophone. My little brother and I shared the same DNA traits as my father, who apparently loved music as well and played the organ in the church. We laughed and continued to get to know each other.

After getting off the phone with my brothers, I felt a little more encouraged. I started sending them messages, wishing them a wonderful weekend or just seeing how their day was going. We even talked about meeting in person. But while my brothers both always responded, they never reached out to me first. I knew these things took time to process, but after several months, I stopped hearing from them. My spirit told me to give it more time, but my mind said, "Give them time? It's been forty-seven years!"

Still, I realized that it wasn't their jobs to work out my problems with my father, who, by the way, had now gone back to being MIA. I was right back to where I started. No father, no phone calls, no cards to say happy birthday. No nothing.

I was upset and sadder than ever. You see, rejection is something I've never been good with, especially when it comes from someone who is close to me. As I am writing this, I am still praying and waiting on change. Maybe one day, my brothers or my father will come see me or invite me to come see them. I know that something is going to give. As I pray and ponder over this situation, I read Psalms 46:10: "Be still and know that I am God; I will be exalted among the heathen, I will be exalted in the earth."

I pray and ask God to give me patience, peace, and, most of all, forgiveness. I need to let go of the resentment I feel towards my father and move on. During these times, I pray Psalms 103:12 ("As far as the east is from the west, so far hath he removed our transgressions from us") and Mark 11:25 ("And when you stand praying, if you hold anything against anyone, forgive them, so that your Father in heaven may forgive you your sins"). I constantly ask God to forgive me at the same measurement as I forgive.

In addition to forgiveness, I also now pray for my own comfort and self-love. I deserve resolution and gratification so that I can move on and make the feelings of loss and yearning go away for good. And God hears me and He provides for me: today, all the love I need comes from own my family and the Father in heaven who will never leave me nor forsake me.

All things are to be for the glory of God.

# Get in Agreement

YOLANDA DOUTHIT

When you come into agreement with another person about God's purpose on earth, the combined results are powerful. The word "agree" is defined in *The Amplified Bible* as "agree and harmonize together or make a symphony together." The word "symphony" is defined as "all available instruments in harmony." A prayer of agreement is one of the most effective forms of prayer. When we pray in agreement, it brings our spirit, mind, and actions into alignment with the powerful Word of our Father. This help us understand and agree that God's Word is true, which is an ideal situation to be in, since we then position ourselves to see the manifestation of God's Will come to pass through Christ Jesus.

When a husband and a wife come together in unity and harmony in prayer, a whole lot can happen. My marriage has surely benefited from praying in agreement. My union has been tested and tried by everything from job losses to infertility. Infertility was the greatest challenge. We've desired to have children for thirteen years and have dealt with the complications for quite some time. It's caused devastating emotions within our marriage—wanting to bear a child for your husband but not being able to do so can create a wedge in any relationship.

My husband and I were married in 2004 but our fertility challenges began well before we were married. In April 2001, I had major health issues, mainly feeling immense pain during and after my menstrual cycles. I gained an enormous amount of weight in a short period of time, especially in my lower abdomen, and I was exhausted all of the time. I went back and forth to the doctor, but my general practitioner was at a loss as to why I was in such pain. I had numerous pregnancy tests and various types of blood work done before he referred me to an OBGYN.

The day I was first told that I had uterine fibroids was a day that is forever etched in my mind. A sonogram revealed several fibroids in and around my uterus. The first thought that came to me was, would I be able to have children? Here I was, twenty-seven-years-old and looking infertility in the face. By the time I received a complete diagnoses of how the fibroids were affecting my fertility health, it was September and I am unable to work. I had to be written out of work since the slightest activities caused me such great pain.

Thankfully, the OBGYN I was referred to was astounding. We sat down and made a game plan to preserve my fertility health. He would first perform a laparoscopy to see if he could remove the tumors through small incisions in and around my navel, and if that didn't work, he would perform a myomectomy to remove the fibroids. This procedure was equivalent to having a C-section. On October 2001, I had seven fibroids removed, the largest the size of a grapefruit. He was unable to remove all of them since two were embedded in my uterus. He stated that removing these two would have caused too much damage to my uterus and left scar tissue, which would increase the chances of infertility. The two that remained were very small and did not cause any pain or bleeding. My doctor noted that there was minimal damage done to my uterus and that there was possibility that I could still have children.

I spent four days in the hospital and eight weeks in recovery. I was so thankful and grateful to God that my surgery was a success. It was an arduous journey to healing but Monte was with me every step of the way. He was at my side before, after, and during my recovery, praying with and for me. Three years later in 2004, we married with our eyes set on building a family. Then it happened again.

I became ill in September 2009. After another series of tests, it was determined that I had ten large fibroid tumors that were causing even more intense pain and weight gain, and I was unable to work again. We were, again, faced with the possibility of infertility. At this time, I had been married for five years and was seeking assistance with my fertility issue. I went through many disheartening appointments with physicians in Georgia (where we were living at the time) who immediately recommended a hysterectomy since they were concerned about excessive bleeding during yet another myomectomy. They were also concerned as to how they would preserve my reproductive organs because there were so many large tumors. These were not the options we wanted hear. We desired children, and I felt defeated. But Monte felt that there was hope for us and he encouraged me to call my physician in Charlotte, North Carolina who performed my first surgery.

I wasn't sure if this would be an option with our insurance and so many other negative thoughts ran through my mind. So we decided to pray and ask God for direction as to what we should do. That's when we came together in prayer and we received the answer. We first called our insurance company to see what our benefits allowed since our insurance was offered through Monte's part time job. We received the unbelievable news that we were covered to see my doctor in North Carolina and also covered to tackle our infertility issues.

Even with this great news, this time was so very hard for us since I was dealing with a multitude of emotions. I had gained so much weight in my abdomen that I could no longer wear my clothes. Ironically, I was forced to shop in maternity stores, which was heartbreaking. This ordeal caused such an emotional strain that, despite my usual joyful spirit, I was depressed. That's when I knew that I was going to require more to win this battle again.

After several meetings with my doctor in Charlotte and a series of test to determine my fertility health, the doctor decided that it would be in my best interest if he performed a myomectomy with a renowned reproductive endocrinologist who would be there to preserve my reproductive organs. After putting this strategy in place, I knew I would need more spiritual reinforcements this time around. I went into my sanctuary, my prayer room, to seek revelation on how to bring healing to my body and defeat this assault on my womb. After much prayer, I received instructions that I was to anoint my womb with oil and to pray in agreement with Monte for my healing everyday until my surgery. I was then given this prayer to share with Monte:

*Heavenly Father, we believe Your Word is settled in heaven and established on earth, and we know that, without faith, it is impossible to please You. We are thankful for the advances in medicine regarding fertility but we are not moved by the doctor's negative report because our faith is not in the wisdom of man, but in the power of You. Your Word says that, whatever we ask in prayer, if we believe it, we will receive it. You said that You would take all sickness away from me, according to Deuteronomy 7:15.*

*We will not cast away our confidence, which has a great reward, but we will be patient because Your Words says that, after we have done Your Will, we will receive the promise of healing. We speak to my body in the Name of Jesus; we will come into alignment and agreement with the Word of God. Every organ and tissue in my body and my husband's body will function in the perfection to which God created them to function.*

*I plead the Blood of Jesus over my womb and reproductive organs. There is no weapon of warfare designed shall remain against us. Creator of the universe, You fearfully and wonderfully made us, and Your Word assures us that You will bless the fruit of my womb. Neither myself nor my husband shall be barren, according to Deuteronomy 7:12-14. You, God, are not a man that You should lie. You have spoken and You always make it good, according to Numbers 23:19.*

*We bless Your Name, Lord, for You have promised and You shall not put us to shame as we wait for You to accomplish Your Word. Until then, we will hold fast to our confession without wavering for we know that He who promised is faithful.*

We followed these instructions until my scheduled surgery. Two days before, Monte and I prayed this prayer over my swollen womb and something unusual occurred. As we anointed my womb, we could feel my abdomen turn cold to the touch. I began to feel a tingling throughout my lower abdomen; we knew that this was confirmation to our prayers that God was with us.

The following day, we went to the hospital to do the pre-surgery check-in and we met with the anesthesiologist. As he was going over the questionnaire, he stopped mid-sentence and said to us, "My wife and I prayed for you last night." Monte and I paused and looked at each other. We couldn't believe that, in this professional environment, the anesthesiologist stated that he and his wife had prayed for us. They agreed in prayer about us! We knew that this was more confirmation, especially because I had major concerns about being placed under sedation. We understood unequivocally that our Father had us covered.

March 23, 2009, I underwent my second myomectomy to remove uterine fibroids. Instead of the ten tumors from the earlier sonograms, they found twenty-four large fibroid tumors when they went in. This explained the constant pain and massive weight gain that I experienced. But the good report was that all of the fears of the other doctors were not part of my surgery story. They were astonished that I had minimum bleeding; the surgery was done under two hours, and I was alert and ready to eat once the sedation wore off. The prayer of agreement worked and God's power showed remarkably.

Throughout this ordeal my relationship with Monte was tested, but again, he was there before, during, and after the ordeal. We stood together on this Word. We witnessed the power of God in the tribulations of birthing a seed. Having to deal with such an intimate subject as having a baby will cause sparks to fly in more ways than one, but we learned that the key to keeping this union intact is to pray in agreement. And He has been in the midst with us!

*Truly, I say to you, whatever you bind on earth shall be bound in heaven, and whatever you loose on earth shall be loosed in heaven. Again I say to you, if two of you agree on earth about anything they ask, it will be done for them by my Father in heaven. For where two or three are gathered in my name, there am I among them.*

—Matthew 18:18-20

What I believe the Father and Christ are trying to tell us with the particular wording in this passages is that there is tremendous power when a group of believers unite together in harmony and in agreement—the impossible will happen. The power produced in a unity prayer will be proportionately greater as more people pray. The more God's people pray together, the more significant the results; the power generated is multiplied. This is what Jesus meant when he said that, if you get into harmony and agree together, He would be in the midst of you.

On May 12, 2016, I again was diagnosed with uterine fibroids. Monte and I are still in agreement that the impossible will happen. The reports from the doctors are grim and hopeless since the uterine tumors have come back more aggressively, but we don't believe their reports. We entered into the sanctuary to find His ways and to read His report on how to bring healing again to my body and how to triumph over this assault for good!

We will be blessed with our seeds and we are we are uniting our tongues and declaring His Word. We are sure that, if we continue to stand and pray in agreement together, no good thing will be withheld from us.

## Prayer of Womb Warfare

*Jesus bore the curse for me; therefore, I forbid growths and tumors to inhabit my body. Growths and tumors have no right in my body, and they are a thing of the past. I am delivered from the authority of darkness that tried to prevail. The life of God within me dissolves growths and tumors, and my strength and health is restored.*

*Your Word became flesh. You sent Your Word to heal me; therefore, my emotions are healed and You will give me strength. Your Word has manifested in my body, causing growths to disappear. Because Your Word has become a part of me, the spirit of depression cannot overtake me. The Spirit is flowing in my bloodstream, every cell of my body restoring and transforming. Every organ and tissue of my body functions in the perfection it was created for and I declare that there will be no malfunctions in my body, in Jesus' Name. Your Life is energizing every cell of my body.*

*Father, we are in agreement that I will no longer need surgery and every tumor will go! Sickness will flee! Tumors will not live in me, for the Spirit of God is upon me and the Word of God is within me. Our marriage will be strengthened even more and the love of God and our love for each other will be manifested even more. Father, You will bring us lasting victory and we will triumph over this enemy—forever. In Jesus' Name, Amen.*

# About the Authors

**Rev. Bernice Parker-Jones** is an anointed preacher, teacher, inspirational speaker, and seeker of the downtrodden and broken-hearted. She received her master of divinity from Howard University in 1993 and was ordained in the African Methodist Episcopal Church in Washington, D.C. She is the founder of the Positive Single Adult Living Ministry (PSALM) and Autumn Leaves, a senior's ministry. She is also a pastor at the Faith Presbyterian Church and an adjunct faculty member at Wesley Theological Seminary.

Parker-Jones is a retired federal government manager who has received several humanitarian and leadership awards. She is also a contributing author to *Many Voices: Multicultural Responses*, published 1994 through University Press of America. Wife to her loving and supportive husband, Elder Edward Jones, Sr., a mother of two daughters and one son, and a grandmother of two granddaughters and five grandsons.

**Tonya Barbee** has served in the educational field all of her adult life. She earned her BS and MBA from National-Louis University in Chicago, Illinois, and has been working at the National Defense University as a project manager since 2004.

Barbee has been featured in "My LYFF Story," "Turning Up the Gospel," "Goodreads," "Joyous Word," "Renee Wiggins' Blog Radio Show," "Push-IT News," "Scoop USA Newspaper," Ernest Armstrong with "Say Your Peace" Radio, Jeff Foxx Radio, WBGR with Lionel Green, Daulton Anderson of WHCR, and "Black News." In 2014, she published her first book, *The Little Girl Inside: Owning My Role in My Own Pain*. She's working on two new projects.

Barbee is a native of Durham, North Carolina. She has four children—Drew, Jessica, Christian, and Zachary—and seven grandchildren. As a member of the First Baptist Church of Highland Park, she remains active with both her church and community.

Learn more at: www.iamstillarose.com

**LuDrean Peterson** is the CEO and founder of Delivering On Ideas & Thoughts (DO IT). She holds a MBA and a master of science in management (MSM) with an emphasis in human resources management. She has twenty-six-years of experience in human resources and sixteen years as an office director and hiring manager. She specializes in the areas of organizational and career development, strategy and advisory services in the workplace, mentoring, resume-writing, and interview preparation. She helps others live out their dreams, professionally and personally, by providing effective resources and tools. For her work, she received the FDA Pioneer Award for achieving groundbreaking success.

Learn more at www.do-it-delivers.com

**Marian Currie** is a motivational speaker, mentor, and thirty-year program manager for the federal government. She is the founder and CEO (Chief Encouragement Officer) of S.H.O.E. Girl Inc., a non-profit organization dedicated to mentor girls, between the ages of 9-18, creating opportunities for them to respect themselves and others through workshops, seminars, and self-development activities. Known as the firm, yet loving mentor "Ms. C," she has received accolades and recognition from parents, teachers, and community service organizations.

Currie resides in the Washington, D.C., area and has two children. In her spare time, she loves to read, journal, write poetry, listen to music, cook, and spend quality time with her family.

**Ruby Mabry** is a bestselling author, CEO of New Life Manor, Inc., thought leader, and empowerment coach. She is also the founder of Live on Purpose Movement through which she unites, inspires, and empowers women to live their true purpose in life and in business. Her leadership has been recognized by her peers, social workers, and the Agency for Persons with Disabilities. She has been featured on "Mom Talk Radio nationally syndicated radio show for moms," "WOKB-1680 AM Radio, "Peace On The Streets," "iHeart Radio, The Conversation," *Entrigue Magazine, Gigare' Lifestyle Magazine*, and *EIN Presswire* The Best of Autumn Reading 2016. Mabry also has over twenty-five years in healthcare administration, nursing, and medical transcription. Mabry lives in Orlando, Florida with her family. She is also a retired United States Army wife, who is married to her high school sweetheart of twenty-nine years. They have two beautiful children. She enjoys spending quality time with her family, listening to music, traveling, writing, watching movies, and living life to the fullest.

To learn more, visit www.liveonpurposemastermind.com

**Milton Dickerson** was born in Washington, D.C. A product of a single family home and the only boy of six sisters, he spent his teenage years in North Carolina, which left a significant impact on him. He graduated from North Carolina Central University, earning a degree in history. For the past decade, he taught history for various grades and ages.

Dickerson is the founder of MOimpact, a motivational speaking company. He has lectured on various topics such as race, black church, black males, and education at various venues such as seminars and church functions.

In his spare time, Dickerson enjoys watching documentaries, reading, and doing speaking engagements. This contribution will be his freshman work.

Reach him via email at modickerson83@gmail.com
and on Twitter via @professor_keys

**Rev. Allison G. Daniels** is a native of Washington, D.C. She holds an associate degree in business administration and is currently pursuing her bachelor degree in business administration. She has over thirty-one years of legal experience in the federal government. She is also a certified life coach and diversity trainer for women's issues with the Professional Woman Network (PWN).

Daniels is also a motivational speaker and an accomplished author of over thirty-one books and is now an award-winning, bestselling author of her book, *Walk in your Authority: Unleashing the Divine Power from Within*. Her mission is to help empower women who seek professional and personal growth through venues that provide motivation, awareness, and mentoring. She teaches discipleship, stewardship and servant leadership through networking, teaching, mentoring, workshops, conference, and more.

Learn more at www.allisongdaniels.com or email at allisongdaniels@verizon.net

**Roz Knighten-Warfield** is known as a smiling prayer champion who passionately creates relational currency among women who desire to lead lives full of zeal, clarity, and courage. She is a certified power coach of Coach Academy International and shares writings with other women of influence such Anna McCoy and Thelma Wells. Her first devotional, #StopIt! & SMILE, encourages people to stop lower-nature thinking that causes negativity and to SMILE, Simply Make Intentional Love Encounters ™. She, alongside visionary Cheryl Polote-Williamson, is also an Amazon bestselling coauthor of the book *Soul Source* and was featured on TBN Tulsa KDOR-17 with Pastor Marcus Howard.

Knighten-Warfield is married to Vincent Warfield. They have three children and two grandchildren, and they reside in Dallas, TX.

Learn more at www.stopitsmile.com

**Tina Mayo-Hunter** was born and raised in Arlington, Virginia. She is a businesswoman, wife, mother of two daughters and one son, and a grandmother of two. She is the owner of ME! Foundation and Smoochez Boutique, through which she motivates and empowers women and young girls to live their best lives. She encourages friends and family to be fearless and not let anyone or anything stand in your way of doing what makes them happy.

Learn more at Tinahuntermotivate@gmail.com

**Veronica Howard** is a two-time cancer survivor, a proud mother of two beautiful children, a grandmother to one grandson, and a woman of God who steps out on faith. She graduated from Strayer University in 2006 with an associate degree in Business Administration, and, today, she is a station manager for the Washington Metropolitan Area Transit Authority, the second largest rail system in the world. She is also the administrator of the Cancer Support Ministry at Mt Ennon Baptist Church in Clinton, Maryland, through which she mentors audiences, friends, coworkers, and family members who are currently fighting cancer. She stands firmly on God's word. Howard resides in Oxon Hill, Maryland.

Contact her via email at Howardveronica41@yahoo.com

**Yolanda Douthit** is a dedicated wife to Monte Douthit and a "Preacher's Kid" who has been grounded in faith and taught strong values that have been influential in several churches and ministries throughout her life. In 2012, she founded the Sanctuary Ministries, which educates and services those who are seek a deeper, more purposeful relationship with the Creator. She was ordained into ministry in 2014 by her mother, and earned her bachelors of science in religious studies in May 2015 and her masters of arts in global studies in May 2017 from Liberty University. She is currently pursuing her doctorate. She embraces the dual call of preaching and teaching as she operates in her gifts in The Sanctuary Weekly.

Learn more at www.yolandadouthit.com

**Shani McIlwain** is an author, business owner, radio host, wife, mother, and woman of God. Her administrative support company, Practical Partners, assists authors, coaches, and speakers in bringing their visions to fruition. Her books—*Sharing My Mess: 90 Days of Prayer and Spiritual Intimacy with God* and *It's Time to Make a Change: 30 Days to Renew Your Mind, Heart, and Soul*—provide women with daily practices that will help them develop everlasting relationships with God. In addition to her work, McIlwain volunteers her time and skills at N Street Village Women's Shelter, Central Union Mission, and Standing Tall for Our Children.

McIlwain lives in Washington, D.C., with her husband and four children. When she isn't writing or serving, she enjoys reading, traveling, and watching movies.

To learn more, visit her website at
www.sharingwithshani.com

# Sources

Unless otherwise indicated, scripture quotations are from the Holy Bible, King James Version. All rights reserved.

Scriptures marked MSG are taken from The Message®. Copyright © 1993, 1994, 1995, 1996, 2000, 2001, 2002. Used by permission of NavPress Publishing Group.

Scriptures marked NIV are taken from the New International Version®. Copyright © 1973, 1978, 1984, 2011 by Biblica, Inc.™. All rights reserved.

Scriptures marked NKJV are taken from the New King James Version®. Copyright © 1982 by Thomas Nelson. All rights reserved.

Scriptures marked NLT are taken from the New Living Translation®. Copyright © 1996, 2004, 2007, 2013 by Tyndale House Foundation. All rights reserved.

## CREATING DISTINCTIVE BOOKS
## WITH INTENTIONAL RESULTS

We're a collaborative group of creative masterminds with a mission to produce high-quality books to position you for monumental success in the marketplace.

Our professional team of writers, editors, designers, and marketing strategists work closely together to ensure that every detail of your book is a clear representation of the message in your writing.

### Want to know more?
Write to us at info@publishyourgift.com
or call (888) 949-6228

Discover great books, exclusive offers, and more at
**www.PublishYourGift.com**

Connect with us on social media

@publishyourgift

www.ingramcontent.com/pod-product-compliance
Lightning Source LLC
Chambersburg PA
CBHW071521080526
44588CB00011B/1519